Praise for *Beyond UX Des*

"Finally, someone's talking about the hidden truths of UX! What UXers have to face to thrive in their careers (and keep their sanity)!"

- Adam Fard
Founder UX Pilot

"A solid primer into the unseen work that often goes unnoticed behind pretty pixels."

- Taylor Palmer
Head of Design @ Productable | Co-Founder UX Tools

"This book is an absolute game changer from how it's written to the practical analogies it uses. I love that it's not the ordinary things you hear people talk about, but actually, what happens in large or small teams."

- Denis Jeliazkov
Founder UI Learn

"This book will be my career companion for many years to come... it covers it all! It dives into the things I wish I would have known as a Junior Designer but also a great refresher on navigating the industry as a Senior."

- Christopher Nguyen
Founder UX Playbook

"Jeremy teaches us everything he knows in an enjoyable conversational style that we have grown to love from his podcast. I believe this book offers help to anyone wanting a real-life view into the world of UX."

- Lennart Nacke, PhD
Professor of UX Design & Research

"What I love about Jeremy's approach to UX is that it's rooted in what actually happens with design decisions inside an organization. This is a practical guide for UX pros who want to move with confidence through their projects and careers.

- Lex Roman
Founder Growthtrackers and Low Energy Leads

Praise for *Beyond UX Design*

"Jeremy's book is an epic compass for any design professionals: it is about 'being more than designers'. There are politics, storytelling, content creation, facilitation and so many other skills you need to master. I can't recommend this book enough, it'll help you navigate the complexity of our design profession."

- Krisztina Szerovay
Product designer & consultant | Mentor @10X Designers

"Beyond UX Design is a great book for anyone interested in design. As the title suggests, it goes beyond screens and Figma and discusses how these principles fall into users' minds. Easy to understand and full of useful ideas, it's a must-read for designers."

- Balint Bogdan
Author The Psychology Behind Design

"If you're a UX or Product Designer, then you know there is infinite advice online these days. With so many opinions, it can be hard to cut through the fluff and identify actionable advice that actually works in your career. Jeremy's book is one of the most straightforward, down to earth, actionable guides I know of."

- Mitchell Clements
Sr. Product Design Manager

"Years of experience in UX compressed in a well-written, actionable book you'll find handy whether you are a junior or senior designer. Jeremy did an excellent job capturing all the knowledge he gained over the years and now offers you the opportunity to advance your career in lightspeed."

- Filip Gres
Creator of GriddyIcons

"Having an overview of what UX is about is great for starters. Jeremy goes above and beyond giving this insight. The book gives an idea of the entire space, including practical ideas I'll use myself, especially taking ownership."

- Thijs Kraan
Design Content Consultant at Value Positioner

BEYOND UX DESIGN

Master Your Craft Beyond Pixels & Prototypes

Jeremy Miller

Foreword by
Tom Greever
Author of Articulating Design Decisions

Beyond UX Design: *Master Your Craft Beyond Pixels and Prototypes*

Self Published

Published 2024.

Available online at:
www.beyondUXdesign.com

ISBN: 979-8-9902341-0-9

To my wonderful wife Aimee
for the unconditional support, and for putting up
with my long nights and weekends getting this done.

This wouldn't have happened without you.

Hi there.
I'm Jeremy!

I'm Jeremy, a designer with nearly two decades in the design industry and the voice behind the "Beyond UX Design" podcast.

I strongly believe that soft skills are what will make you a truly effective UX professional, and ultimately, that you can't build great software without great relationships.

Once you're done reading this book, I hope you'll believe the same.

Cheers!
Jeremy

Table of Contents

Foreword   xv

Introduction   2

Chapter 01

Understanding Our Role and Its Impact   12

What is UX Design?   14

The UX team doesn't own problem-solving   22

Our job is often about influence   23

What about the rest of the team?   24

Chapter 02

The Right Context Makes Our Jobs Easier   28

First, your first job is to get up to speed   29

Think of your job as a game   33

Don't push your agenda too early   42

Context is king   45

Chapter 03

Building Great Software with Great Relationships   46

Great relationships make our life easier   48

A relationship allegory   49

The benefits of great relationships   53

Building great relationships   54

Great relationships need nurturing   59

Build empathy for your team   64

Have an open-door policy   65

Chapter 04

Simplify Your Work With Internal Networking   68
The benefits of internal networking   70
Internal networking tips   82
Networking will serve you for years to come   89

Chapter 05

Survive and Thrive in a VUCA World   90
What is VUCA?   92
VUCA isn't one thing but four distinct things   95
Charting the VUCA scenarios   97
Thrive in volatility   100
Thrive in uncertainty   106
Thrive in complexity   112
Thrive in ambiguity   118
Courageous followership is critical for success   124
VUCA is not just for leadership training   125

Chapter 06

The Art of Stakeholder Management   126
So, what exactly is stakeholder management?   128
Who are our stakeholders?   128
Why is stakeholder management critical?   132
The UX team's role   134
Assessment tools and frameworks   136
Strategies for good stakeholder relationships   150
Stakeholders are not enemies to fight with   158

Chapter 07

Dealing with The Challenges of Low Design Maturity   160

Low design maturity is not an IC's responsibility   164

Understanding design maturity   165

What does low design maturity mean for UX teams?   168

Tips to improve your situation   170

Common scenarios and how to deal with them   172

Sometimes, these strategies won't work   191

Chapter 08

The Value of Courageous Followership   194

What is followership?   196

Why is followership important?   198

Characteristics of a good follower   199

The vital role of UX professionals as followers   207

Turn followership into leadership success   211

Acknowledgments   215

My design work was practically secondary to my ability to get other people to support it.

-Tom Greever

Foreword

"Why don't you just work your magic?"

This is how a colleague ended a meeting with me at one of my first design jobs. It didn't seem cringe to me at the time the way that it does now. For one, I knew he was just saying he didn't really know what he wanted or needed - and that was fine because it was my job as a designer to make those decisions, right? But also, my work did feel a little bit like magic. I did have special skills. I could create things that others couldn't. I had spent time learning tools, honing my craft, and understanding users. After spending years working to become good at design, it felt appropriately indulgent to consider myself a bit of a magician. At the time, I thought that was the primary value that I provided: creating design.

I've since learned that I was wrong. Just because he didn't know what he wanted didn't mean it was my job to make the design decisions on my own. It meant I should have taken the time to dig deeper and truly understand his needs, which ultimately would have revealed more about the business and customers. I didn't do that because I thought my job was to create the design. Naturally, when I came back with a revision, he didn't "like" that one either and the cycle started over. It turns out there's nothing magic about using my skills to make what I think are well-informed decisions only to have them overridden by someone else. Maybe the design wasn't the most valuable part.

You might think this is a pretty superficial example of a design process gone wrong. After all, in the years since that conversation, the UX and design industry has come a long way.

There are more opportunities to learn UX than ever before. Many companies have embraced a design-driven mentality, adopting agile-like approaches and matrixed teams. Even though it seems like everyone should understand the value of design by now, that's not always the case. Product owners want to skip user testing because of a deadline, executives continue to push their pet projects, and developers prefer their existing components over our new design.

It often seems like other people simply don't understand design: our process and the value we bring. We're often asked to cut corners and skip steps, so it's natural to want to stand up for our principles by insisting on doing things right. If we just got everyone to follow the right steps, then maybe they would see the value of design. So we ask the five whys, we lay out our process in detail, we explain why sales can't do real research, and we make sure everyone diverges before they converge. Doing things right becomes our mantra, and before long, people are exhausted by working with us. A narrow-minded focus on craft at all costs has turned us into rigid, difficult people to work with. Maybe the design process wasn't the most valuable part either.

It was about this point in my career when I began looking beyond the pixels of my day-to-day to better understand what it would take to be successful in the design industry. I saw that there were really talented designers who couldn't get support for their work simply because they weren't good at explaining their decisions to other people. Often times, people who weren't designers at all were more likely to get their way if they had better relational capital with the people in charge. It didn't seem fair, but it got me to thinking. Maybe the most valuable part had nothing to do with design skill at all.

During this thought experiment, it occurred to me that I could have the most innovative design in the world, but if I wasn't able to get the support I needed from the people around me, it would never see the light of day. In that way, it almost didn't matter how good my work was. My design work was practically secondary to my ability to get other people to support it. What would make me successful as a designer would be my ability to work with others, build relationships, and earn their trust.

I had spent so many years trying to improve my craft, while neglecting the thing that would truly make me effective and allow me to get more done. Design was only a small part of the job. Relationships mattered more because they were critical to understanding the larger context in which I worked. Having good relationships made it easier for me to get approval of my designs. Being pragmatic and flexible with my approach actually made it easier to influence the process going forward. Improving my soft skills ultimately improved my design work too because I had higher levels of engagement from other people on the team. It's something I wish I had known earlier in my career.

The good news is, you don't have to make the same mistakes I did. By reading this book, you'll be much better prepared to handle these challenges. Whether you're just starting out or have been around design for a while, the practical advice in these pages will help you approach your work in a more productive way. Your craft and process are important, but to be truly successful as a designer, you have to look beyond UX design.

Tom Greever
Author of Articulating Design Decisions

Introduction

Are you a seasoned UX veteran
or a recent design grad?

You may be on the hunt for the latest
design trends, UX research best
practices, accessibility principles, the
latest UI and AI tips, or new techniques
for building micro-interactions in
whatever the newest tool du jour is...

While I may not have the latest design
trends or UI tips, I do have something
equally valuable for your UX journey.

So buckle up!

I'd like to introduce myself

What's up, UX fam? How's your mom and them? My name is Jeremy. My friends call me JMills. My kids call me Dad. My wife calls me whatever the hell she wants. And my dog just stares at me funny when he wants to go outside.

I can't tell you how excited I am to have you join me on this little adventure we are about to embark on.

I sincerely believe that this book will provide practical advice to help anyone struggling to advance in their career, to avoid some of the pitfalls I fell for when I started nearly 20 years ago. God, it's wild to write that down. Where has the time gone? But with this book, you'll be well-prepared for the challenges ahead.

The tagline for this book is "Master Your Craft Beyond Pixels and Prototypes." You might ask yourself, "Jeremy, what are you talking about? What does that even mean?" Let me explain.

A couple of years ago, I started mentoring designers. I have been fortunate enough to meet with designers from all over the world, both aspiring and veterans. Through those meetings, I quickly noticed a trend.

That trend is they are laser-focused on hard skills. They are generally speaking, obviously. Not everyone was like this, but it was enough for me to notice.

This trend manifests itself in many of the portfolios I see online and in conversations about process and operations that I have. Many designers focus exclusively on hard skills. Their case studies and processes look like a checklist: I did this, I did this, I did this, I did this—BOOM great software.

It's as if these designers are ticking boxes:

- ✓ Interviews. Check.
- ✓ Personas. Check.

✓ Journey map. Check.

✓ Wireframes. Check.

✓ Usability study. Check.

Doing these things is all well and good. However, we need to understand how and why these activities will result in a great user experience.

Something I say all the time is: *"You're more than a designer."*

Here's what I mean by that:

In school, books, boot camps, and especially on social media and online, we're often taught an ideal scenario—a happy path for how we should do design—a specific order of things. We do those things in the correct order, and somehow, an app is made.

Take the classic Double Diamond, for instance.

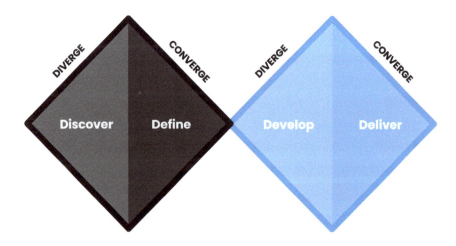

If you follow this process from A to B, start to finish, you will have a great user experience.

But here's the thing: It is very rarely how things work in the real world. In the real world, you may pick up where others left off.

Your team will ask you to skip some steps. Your team will ask you to decide before you have all the answers. And we have to deal with people–A lot of people. And that makes building great software extremely hard.

You may have heard some of these stereotypes: the pushy stakeholder with unrealistic expectations, the product manager who can't say no to the pushy stakeholder, the manager who gives unrealistic deadlines, the QA engineer who always misses UX issues, and the software engineer who just wants to code in the dark alone with a two-liter of Mountain Dew.

If you've encountered those stereotypes, the hard skills you've mastered–or working to master right now–won't matter, I promise. What will matter are the skills and techniques we'll cover in this book.

What is "craft?"

I hear lots of people talking about the importance of "craft" on an almost daily basis. Craft is essential, but it's an odd conversation. Craft is often positioned as the alternative to something else. You either focus on "craft," or you focus on... Whatever the alternative is, I'm not sure.

Unfortunately, the term "craft" has been co-opted as another argument to pitch designer against designer. It's become another way for us to create more in-groups and out-groups. From my perspective, we have a hard enough time doing great work. Conversations like these are never helpful.

From the perspective of non-designers, "craft" is often seen as the deliverables. Craft is the tangible thing that stakeholders can see and interact with. It's often the result of those hard skills mentioned a moment ago.

You're more than a designer, because there's more to UX than design.

But craft is much more. Mastering the craft of user experience is more than just the hard skills of figuring out what font pairings and color schemes work best together. It's more than determining the proper placement of elements on the page. Craft is more than perfecting micro-interactions or using design systems efficiently. Craft is more than creating any one specific artifact or deliverable.

Craft is also staying calm during meetings with a difficult Product Manager. Craft is managing stakeholder expectations and finding the best path forward. Craft is also helping the team understand how they contribute to a user's overall experience and influencing decisions when the time comes.

Craft goes far beyond "design." In this industry, you're more than a designer and you need to master your craft beyond pixels and prototypes. There is more to this job than simply creating tangible deliverables.

Sometimes, we have to be more than designers.

- ✓ We need to be facilitators and relationship builders.
- ✓ We need to be influencers and storytellers.
- ✓ We need to be politicians and diplomats.
- ✓ We need to be students and teachers.
- ✓ We need to be leaders and followers.

So, in this book, we won't discuss essential hard skills. Lots of people have already done a great job of doing that.

In this book, we will discuss all the different skills that help turn those necessary deliverables into real value for end users and your business, like how to network most effectively within your organization, build great relationships with your team, influence stakeholders and decision-making, deal with the uncertainty of teams with low design maturity, and shut up and take a back seat when it's appropriate. These are the soft skills, or better yet, foundational skills, that are often overlooked. However, these skills are crucial for a successful career in UX.

At the end of the day, a well-thought-out interactive prototype with all the delightful micro-interactions might be beautiful and impressive. Still, that design is only as valuable as your team's ability to build it and into a user's hands.

In conjunction with the essential hard skills, the skills we'll talk about in this book will be what help make that happen.

It's nearly impossible to tackle the mind-numbingly tricky work of building and releasing high-quality software to users if we focus only on the hard skills and completely ignore the importance of these foundational skills.

In my years of experience, I've seen UX teams get much more done with "soft skills" than with hard skills alone. There is so much more to this job than simply design. We need to leverage those foundational skills if we ever hope to improve the lives of our end users and our careers, for that matter.

Now, with all that said, I want this to be abundantly clear–Those hard skills that make you good at your craft are critical. If you need help understanding the fundamentals, if you don't understand the rules, the laws, the tools, or if you don't know how to do the job, these so-called soft skills won't help you. Remember that.

Think of it like building a house. Hard skills are the foundation and structure that keep the house standing. Soft skills, however, are the comfortable furniture, personal touches, and landscaping that make the space livable. It's what makes your house a home.

But a beautiful interior won't compensate for a weak foundation. Both are important. Hard skills lay the groundwork for soft skills to shine effectively.

I didn't write this book to diminish the hard skills. Yes, those hard skills are fundamental. Many other authors and thought leaders can help you with those things. I do not intend to replace those books or ideas. I wrote this book to help make those other books more impactful to your career.

A note about titles

As we continue to talk about UX design, I think it's worth discussing my perspective on "Product Design" and how that relates to the overall concept of UX design, especially as it relates to the ideas we'll cover in this book.

The title of "Product Design" is more popular now than ever. I don't want to get into a debate about the two because I think the discussion is mostly irrelevant, especially for this book, since focusing on titles is focusing so much on hard skills.

Regardless of what you call yourself or what responsibilities your team gives you, whether you do more or less research, talk to many users, or none at all, the concepts in this book are valuable to help you navigate the complexities of day-to-day work.

For the sake of this book, since we are not focusing on hard skills, you can swap out UX Designer for Product Designer, UX/UI Designer, or even UX Researcher, Product Manager, or Software Engineer for that matter. The concepts in this book are all still perfectly applicable. I'll mostly use the term "UX Professional" in this book, but remember it shouldn't matter.

Mastering the craft of user experience is more than just mastering the hard skills.

Thank you!

Lastly, I am grateful you are giving this book a chance.

There is a ton of UX content available to you. I know you have options, and I can't tell you how much it means to me that you are here, reading, taking a few nuggets of wisdom away, and ultimately improving your work and your career.

I believe in this idea of an Infinite Game that this game of life never ends. There's no finish line. It's not a competition. We're not competing with anyone but ourselves to be better than we were the day before.

Going forward, I hope this book will be part of your library of many excellent books and earn a place next to Tom Greever's Articulating Design Decisions! 😝 I hope this book helps you become a genuinely great but, most importantly, effective UX professional that the rest of your team looks to for guidance.

If this sounds like something you're into, this book is for you.

-After you've read this book, please share it on Slack, LinkedIn, or whenever you get your social media dopamine hit. If you know someone who would get something out of it, please share it.

I'm a small voice in the ocean of UX content, and it means so much to me that you're reading this book.

From the bottom of my heart, thank you! 🙏

Chapter 01

Understanding Our Role and Its Impact

"UX" and "UX Design" are loaded terms.

Depending on who you are and your job title, how you define the term can enormously impact your approach to building software.

More critically, this can play a prominent role in how non-designers approach working with the UX team–for better or worse.

So, in this chapter, we will break it down and set the record straight.

L et's talk about Calendly, a scheduling tool many of us use every day. Have you ever used Calendly? It's a handy app that allows someone to connect a calendar like Google Calendar and set their availability so that other people who want to schedule a meeting with them can see their availability and quickly set up a time to meet where both can make it.

It cuts out all the back-and-forth emails when scheduling a call. I want to set up a meeting with you. I see your availability. I select a time that works for me. Boom. Meeting.

What's interesting about this tool is that the interface works well when I find someone I want to meet with and they send me their Calendly link.

I find a time when we're both available. I hit send, and we meet.

But what happens when I have the Calendly account and try to find someone I want to meet with? What happens if they don't have a Calendly link, but I do? Do I send it to them and ask them to find time to meet with me?

If I reach out to them, what kind of experience will they have with Calendly when they hear from me out of the blue? Then I asked them to do some work so I could meet with them.

In my opinion, here's where something like Calendly completely fails and negatively impacts the experience.

I've had this same situation happen to me. And when it happened, the first thing I thought was, "Wait, you're reaching out to me. You wanted to meet with me. Now you're asking me to do some work for you. To set up a meeting for you to have with me?"

The Calendly team could have done everything by the book. They could have had a solid problem statement, research, design, and usability studies. I'm sure talented designers, researchers, software engineers, product people, etc., worked on this. However, the current state of the tool doesn't account for this one thing, and now, some subset of users have a terrible experience with their product.

I've talked to a few people who adamantly oppose these tools for this very reason. This disconnect means Calendly and similar tools are missing out on business revenue.

I'm raising this example, but to be clear, I don't have a solution. I don't know how to fix this problem, but that's not the point. The point here is to highlight that our role involves investigating and empathizing with every aspect of the user's journey and working with our entire team to holistically address these problems.

Building software involves trade-offs and compromises. In the following chapters, we'll discuss different ways to work within these constraints.

What is UX Design?

Before we dig into the intricacies of navigating and overcoming challenges as a UX professional, let's define 'UX.' But before you skip ahead thinking you already know what UX is, hear me out.

My specific definition of UX will give you a deeper understanding of how I shape my views on the UX profession. It should shed light on how I make decisions about my work as a UX designer, my problem-solving approach, team collaboration, and other aspects of my work. And it will ultimately do the same for you.

How you define 'UX' and 'UX design' can significantly influence the decisions you make in your daily work.

How I define "UX" underscores the importance of collaboration in our work as a team. Therefore, discussing this before we explore the other topics in this book is an essential first step.

What is UX?

This question is often more polarizing than it should be. And honestly, that is unfortunate.

Before I wrote this chapter, I did some digging to understand what was in the zeitgeist. I found some articles where UX Professionals describe the craft as something like: "UX Design is the process teams use" [01] or "UX Design is improving the experience" [02] or something related to empathy for users, which I want to stress is essential. But for me, these things are mostly irrelevant when working with non-designers–especially when they don't align with us on what "UX" means.

I found an article on UserTesting.com that had 15 experts weigh in on what they think UX design is. Only one believed UX was about solving problems, which blew my mind. Only one of them!

So many people in the software industry today automatically equate UX design with UI design. It is as if UX professionals are the evolution of web designers or digital designers. That implies you must be a Dribbble god with the most cutting-edge and trendy UIs to be an effective UX Professional. And that just isn't the case. Excellent visual design skills are only one aspect of our work, albeit an important one.

Many others associate UX design with a specific process where you do a series of things in a particular order as if there is some magical formula for good UX. While process and specific steps are often critical, I have some nuanced feelings about it.

---

01. https://www.usertesting.com/blog/what-is-ux-design-15-user-experience-experts-weigh-in
02. https://www.interaction-design.org/literature/topics/ux-design

What UX design is not

Before defining UX, let's debunk some common misconceptions about what UX is. It's essential to be aware of and counter these misconceptions as they can significantly impact how the rest of our team thinks about what we really do.

There is undoubtedly a process that a team might follow to achieve a great user experience. But this is not "UX." These steps are simply the work of the UX and the larger software team. Mindlessly performing these steps without understanding the user's needs and context is what many call "UX theater."

- ✕ UX is not simply crafting a beautiful interface.
- ✕ UX is not visual design or even UI design.
- ✕ UX is not color theory or typography.
- ✕ UX is not just advocating for users.
- ✕ UX is not about data hierarchy.
- ✕ UX is not mastering Figma.
- ✕ UX is not design systems.

These things can–and will–make or break the user experience, but focusing on these alone will not guarantee a great experience for users.

UX design is about creating meaningful outcomes for users, which means increased revenue for our business. It's crucial always to keep the user's goals in mind. No matter how good other parts of the software are, if the user doesn't get what they expected, it won't result in a positive outcome or experience.

A beautiful app that doesn't do what a user needs it to do is not a good piece of software—end of story.

Most critically, users will not be willing to pay for it.

What UX teams do on their own does not guarantee a good experience.

LET'S HEAR FROM THE EXPERTS

Yaddy Arroyo
Principal Multimodal AI designer

Yaddy shares some important insights about how concepts from improv can make you a better collaborator and team player

YES, AND is an improv philosophy that highlights supporting others' core ideas. But sometimes having to say "no" is the most supportive thing you can do for your colleagues or clients.

The YES, AND philosophy has taken me far in my career because it taught me to actively listen, stay in the present, and go with it!

One of my favorite projects was an AI Social Listening start-up that had an amazing tool only professional data analysts could use. Our C-suite clients couldn't understand the value of our product because it was too complex to use. Having freshly applied my improv skills, I was eager to YES, AND this problem and find a way to create an interface even a CMO could use.

The company had a powerful technology that relied on Boolean logic to slice and dice data in a way that revealed true insights. We interviewed analysts and customer success agents, and all we kept getting told was "There's no way you can do this, it's hard and we're the only ones who can put up with this crap and use this tool day-in and day-out."

Here I was being told by board members, bosses, and clients that we needed to make this tool easier to use, and here I had like 50 analysts poo-pooing on the idea, saying that it would never be possible and to not waste my time. I was between a rock and a hard place. Clients wanted something they could use in-house without the help of our analysts, but our analysts didn't want to lose the powerful functionality they had to make the product simpler for others to use.

So I YES, AND-ED everyone. Why not keep a similar version of the existing UI for the analysts (analyst-view) and create a brand new visual Boolean logic interface for the clients (smart view)?

The creative process for this project was so interesting. When I kept hearing from both sides all of their polarizing requirements (e.g. "it has to be easy to use!!" BUT "It can't lose its complex way of slicing and dicing information" OR "there has to be lots of white space" BUT "we need to be able to zoom in and see verbatim conversations in context"), I could have easily run away but I didn't.

Improv taught me that even when things go wacky, sometimes you just gotta surf that wave and let it take you where it takes you. It led me to a pow-wow with the lead product person who had an amazing UI idea. I YES, AND-ED the heck out of the idea, even if I didn't know all the specifics of how it would work. I sketched it out, drafted conditions, figured out specs, and even pitched it to the front-end devs. They hated it. They said it couldn't work. But like water in a stream, I flowed with it. I started asking them what didn't work about it, and what problems they saw. Instead of NOs, I heard solvable "MEHs."

YES, AND is NOT the same as saying "Yes." What these devs did was push back for good reasons. They had legitimate concerns I hadn't addressed. By saying NO to my initial sketches, they said YES to higher standards. I used their NOs to bulletproof the concepts, and in the end, we had a working prototype that clients loved and analysts appreciated.

So, what is UX design?

Before discussing UX design or what a UX Professional does, let's consider UX more broadly.

Don Norman coined the term "User Experience" in the 90s.

> *"User experience encompasses all aspects of the end-user's interaction with the company, its services, and its products."*

Notice he doesn't mention anything about design, tools, or processes. It's all about the end user's interaction with the company, service, or product.

At its most basic level, UX is the experience that a user has. It's that simple. It's right there in the name!

It's important to remember that when we discuss these other aspects of UX design, we're talking about everything that influences the user's experience. A UX team cannot guarantee that they are independently designing a good user experience. It's just not something they can do alone.

When we talk about design systems, visual design, processes, research, tools, etc., that isn't UX. Those processes inform or contribute to the end experience, good or bad. We use those methods to design the user's experience *as best we can.*

I want you to take away one central point from this chapter: **What we, as UX professionals, do on our own does not entirely make or break a good user experience.** Many other factors outside of our team's direct control will influence a user's experience.

The interface alone does not affect the user's experience.

- ✕ It's the number of bugs.
- ✕ It's the user's internet speed.
- ✕ It's the user's physical environment.

✕ It's the reliability of third-party dependencies.

✕ It's the processing power on the user's machine.

✕ It's the stress the user is under while using your product.

You may have designed the most unique, outstanding, award-winning interface. But if any of those other things go wrong, you'll have a bad user experience.

At its core, we can only improve a user's experience when they can do what they set out to do. If a user can't do that, the experience will be negatively impacted.

I downloaded your software and created an account, but now I can't do what I need to do. Fail.

It doesn't matter how thoughtfully laid out the interface was or how attractive the typography and color scheme were. As a user, you wasted my time.

✕ I downloaded your software, but it had so many bugs and errors that I couldn't get it to do what I needed. Fail.

✕ I downloaded your software, and it's not compatible with my computer or phone. Fail.

✕ I downloaded your software, but it never loaded because my data was slow. Fail.

✕ I downloaded your software, but it doesn't meet my accessibility needs. Fail.

This list can go on and on.

So, a good user experience will only happen when all of these things align, and a user can achieve whatever they expect to be able to achieve. More often than not, our job as a UX team is to align business goals with these user needs.

The UX team doesn't own problem-solving

I've talked with many UX professionals over the years. When discussing a UX team's job, I often hear things like, "We're problem solvers." I've heard this sentiment from everyone, from junior interns to senior leadership.

Wanting to solve problems is a noble endeavor, but something even the most senior designers fail to note is that everyone else on the software team thinks they're solving problems, too.

→ Customer Support teams are solving problems.

→ Software Engineers are solving problems.

→ Program Managers are solving problems.

→ Product managers are solving problems.

→ Product Owners are solving problems.

→ Scrum Masters are solving problems.

→ Sales teams are solving problems.

→ Executives are solving problems.

→ QA teams are solving problems.

The UX team does not have a monopoly on problem-solving. You should stop saying that you solve problems, generally, as if that is some unique selling point of UX teams. It's not.

Simply put, this mindset is patronizing and insulting to the rest of the team. The rest of the team considers themselves problem solvers just as much as the design team.

It's offensive when you approach the rest of these "problem solvers" on your team with this patronizing mindset. Most of our time is spent doing things not necessarily considered "design work" and dealing with many challenging situations and people. You'll make those challenging people and situations that much more difficult to deal with.

Do UX professionals solve problems? Absolutely. But instead of saying, "I like to solve problems," think about the type of problems you'll solve with the UX skillset and tools that product, engineering, or QA teams don't have.

When you approach your work with this perspective, it makes putting up with some of the more unpleasant things we'll discuss in later chapters more bearable. Because, as we all know, this job can be a real pain in the ass sometimes.

Our job is often about influence

I had a bad habit of arguing with my team early in my career. Too often, I would present work, receive feedback I didn't like, and push back. It didn't matter who the person was; I had opinions, and my team was going to hear them.

Even worse, I often found something I didn't like and complained about it. I was under the impression that everyone had to listen to me because I was the UX Designer on the team.

You can guess how many minds I changed by acting this way. Spoiler alert: it wasn't many. I had very little influence.

One significant aspect of our job is to share the knowledge and empathy we've built for the users with our team. It's our job to get everyone on the team to understand and empathize with the users so they all want to build the best damn software they can.

So, when the product team thinks about the next feature, they understand how it will impact the experience. When the QA team tests stories, they want to catch as many issues as possible because they know how they will affect the experience. When there are bugs, when an API breaks, or when other technical problems arise, the engineers want to fix the software because they understand how it will impact the experience.

These conversations and compromises shouldn't be a fight or an ongoing battle between UX and everyone else. Our job is to get them where we need them to be. Throughout this book, we'll discuss how we'll do that.

What about the rest of the team?

One reason I clashed so often with my team was my misguided belief that the UX team was the sole champion of users, that somehow the UX team was the only team capable of improving a user's experience. If we weren't going to do it, who would?

I didn't give my team nearly enough credit, or responsibility for that matter.

As we've defined it, the user's experience is not the sole domain of the UX team. If we define User Experience as "the experience a user has," it becomes the responsibility of everyone on the team–from the stakeholders to the product managers to the software engineers to the QA testers and beyond–to be concerned with the experience a user has.

A Great experience is a team sport

Everyone on the team plays a part in the outcome. Any number of things can impact the experience a user has. It's not just the design. It's not just external factors or context. It's not just the code. It's not one thing. It's all of the things together.

This group effort is why we must work closely with our team, and being an empathetic partner is a significant component of our work. When we do this, we can ensure that all the moving parts of these complex systems work together smoothly.

For instance, if the product team and stakeholders are responsible for understanding business outcomes. They must work with the proper UX professionals to conduct research, document it, and discuss it during whatever meetings they facilitate. It's our responsibility to help them focus on users as they approve roadmaps, look for funding, identify resources, define metrics, and whatever else they might be accountable for.

The software team has to consider users while writing stories, defining technical requirements, designing the architecture, and testing features. It's not about shipping the bare minimum as fast as possible; it's about shipping what is suitable for the user. To be fair, there is often a balance between speed, complexity, and value—and that's okay!

But sometimes, these teams just won't want to improve their work. In *Chapter 7*, we'll explore how to deal with some of these frustrating issues.

Every software team is different. Many teams have different names for various roles, so it's impossible to talk about every role and how it might play some part in the experience a user has. Hopefully, you're getting the picture—that the user's experience is something everyone should care about, not just the UX Professionals or the UX team.

If our team is expected to build great software, it's vital that we, as UX professionals, are not solely responsible for the experience. "UX" is not just the components on the screen, the fonts and colors, the visual design, and the copy on the page. Many variables can affect the user's experience.

A big part of our job is ensuring the other teams understand their role in a great user experience. Genuinely great software teams understand these diverse considerations.

It's not about you

In a field so focused on humans, having high emotional intelligence, or emotional quotient (EQ), is essential. Having high EQ means being attuned to your emotions and those around you. It is understanding and managing your emotions effectively to create positive interactions with your team. If you have low EQ, you've undoubtedly seen how much this can impact your career.

We all know that our ability to empathize with users is important. It's right there in our titles, after all. But I'm often quite surprised, nay shocked, to hear UX professionals with years of experience forget about empathy for the rest of their team.

Emotional intelligence plays a vital role in several key areas:

Team collaboration: Working on a software team means working with cross-functional teams with diverse backgrounds and perspectives. In some cases, this includes working with people from many different cultures and regions worldwide. High EQ helps you navigate these differences and foster a collaborative and respectful working environment. It enables you to understand and value the viewpoints of the people on your team, leading to productive collaborations and an overall higher-performing team.

Stakeholder engagement: Effectively engaging with stakeholders is critical to this job. High EQ enables you to communicate persuasively and sensitively. Some might call it "politicking," but think of it more as weaving the story of how stakeholder goals really do align with user needs and business objectives. High EQ helps you better understand their concerns and motivations and allows you to respond in a way that builds trust over time.

Stakeholder management is so important that I've devoted an entire chapter to it. See *Chapter 6* for an in-depth look.

Handling feedback: Receiving and giving feedback is a constant part of our work. High EQ allows you to handle negative feedback without taking criticism personally. It helps you to provide constructive and supportive feedback to others.

Self-reflection and growth: High EQ involves self-awareness and self-regulation. Awareness of your strengths, weaknesses, and biases helps you continually grow, not just as a designer but as a human being, too. It enables you to manage your reactions and emotions, even in stressful or challenging situations, which come with working on software teams.

If you have high emotional intelligence, you're equipped with the skills to understand and manage emotions effectively–your own and those around you. This ability is crucial in this job, where we often find the most success not in technical skills alone but in understanding the humans we work with daily and building meaningful relationships with them every day.

High emotional intelligence equips us with the skills to effectively manage and understand our emotions and those of others. In our role, we often find the most success in understanding the people we work with daily and building meaningful relationships with them. This interpersonal ability, rooted in emotional intelligence, is just as valuable as technical skills.

I'm still blown away by how often industry veterans overlook emotional intelligence.

Chapter 02

The Right Context Makes Our Jobs Easier

Whether you're a fresh face or a seasoned pro, understanding the lay of the land is crucial.

But let's face it; most teams don't have a well-oiled onboarding machine waiting to spoon-feed you context.

So, how do you transform from the new kid on the block to a valuable team player?

Let's explore how to create your own onboarding roadmap, understand the players and rules of your new environment, and set yourself up for long-term success.

Let's learn how to play the game before you try to change the rules.

An interesting byproduct of having a long, "illustrious" career like mine is the opportunity to work with many different people in many different environments. I've had the opportunity to join many different teams, which meant I spent a lot of time getting up to speed.

In the early days of my career, I expected the teams I was joining to have systems and frameworks to get me up to speed so I could quickly contribute. But I found that this was rarely the case.

If you're lucky, your team will have an established onboarding process, but from my experience, this is uncommon. More often than not, new hires are primarily on their own. Ultimately, this means new hires turn into veterans who still don't fully understand the larger context in which they work.

Even if you're not a new hire, it's never too late for an onboarding do-over. If you've been on the team for years without considering these steps, don't fret. There's always room for improvement, and it's never too late to start.

This chapter serves as your compass in navigating an unstructured onboarding process–or going back and starting over if you've been stumbling along for a while. Following the steps we discuss here will ensure you start on the right foot and quickly become a valuable team member.

Take the information in this chapter and use it to create your own onboarding plan. By setting a checklist and timeline for yourself, you can take control of your integration into the team and ensure a smooth transition.

First, your first job is to get up to speed

The teams I've joined throughout my career had nothing close to a formal onboarding process. It was basically "sink or swim."

I didn't precisely sink. But let's just say I wouldn't win any gold medals for my freestyle stroke.

Instead of taking the time to understand the larger context, I jumped right into the work and designed what I thought was right, only to realize too late that what I had come up with was different from what the team and, sometimes, users needed.

I had no context, and I designed for myself. I hadn't designed for my users, and I certainly hadn't designed for my business.

You won't be paid to be a contributing team member for the first couple weeks of a new job. No, your new job for the first couple of weeks is to learn as much as possible so you can be more effective later. This upfront work is the best way to become a valuable team member.

Your job right now is not to develop solutions, give feedback, or crank out wireframes or prototypes. Sure, you can do those things while onboarding if it makes sense, but you will be a more productive team member if you focus on getting up to speed and understanding the larger context before you start focusing on doing any actual work.

While onboarding, setting a goal, creating a timeline, and focusing on your outcome at the end of this period is essential. This structured approach will keep you on track and ensure you're making progress.

The expected outcomes at the end of a month may be to:

- ✓ Be able to speak to business needs.
- ✓ Be able to talk to the users' needs and their pain points.
- ✓ Understand the team's processes.
- ✓ Understand your responsibilities and deliverables.
- ✓ Understand where you will add value.

If someone stopped you and asked you a question, would you be able to speak intelligently and offer insights? Would they trust your opinions and perspective at the end of this conversation?

Your goal shouldn't be to master these things, be able to change the team's processes, or even influence the team to move in a different direction at the end of a month or two. At the very least, your goal should be to reach a point where you're comfortable and confident enough to speak about it if someone asks you.

If you set a deadline for yourself, you can take those outcomes and work backward to create a timeline and mini-deadlines. This structured approach will help you stay organized and control your onboarding process.

Let's look at a quick example. If you want to be able to do these five things we just mentioned, your list may look like this:

- ☐ I need to meet with the stakeholders.
- ☐ I need to meet with the team leads.
- ☐ I need to meet with the researchers.
- ☐ I need to meet with the product managers.
- ☐ I need to read the onboarding documentation.
- ☐ I need to look through our shared drive and review artifacts.

I have 30 days to get up to speed. That means I have to complete all my 1:1s in two weeks, read through the documentation and artifacts in the following two weeks, and be ready to help my new team deliver a set of wireframes in four weeks.

If this sounds like a lot to do, that's because it is. Break those big, overarching goals into smaller, more digestible chunks. Don't be afraid to ask for help if you need it.

I want to share some great advice I received from a colleague a long time ago: "Don't try to drink from the firehose. Turn your

Think of your job as a game. Get to know the players & the rules.

head a bit, let it splash you in the face, and try to drink some water as it sprays you, but don't expect to swallow it all at once."

Remember that as you embark on this discovery and onboarding adventure, which we discuss in this chapter, you might find that your plan needs to evolve and that you need to pivot. Be prepared to adapt to the new information or insights you uncover.

I've been there before. Just take it slow, but keep moving forward.

Think of your job as a game

Life is a game. It's not a finite game like checkers, chess, or football. Life is an infinite game. An infinite game is a game where there are no fixed players and no fixed rules. The objective of an infinite game isn't to win. It's to keep playing as long as possible.[01]

And that is essentially life, isn't it?

I like to think of work in the same way.

→ There are people we work with. These are the players.

→ There are processes, roles, tasks, etc. These are the rules.

Our goal is to keep going until we retire or win the Powerball jackpot. There isn't an official ending.

Chances are good your team has created pages and pages of documentation. The product team has likely created Product Requirement Documents (PRDs) and competitive analyses, and they may have done lots of market research and saved those findings somewhere. Likely roadmaps and milestones are wasting away in a shared drive somewhere.

Software engineers have likely created various data schema maps and technical specifications. There are likely things to read from previous sprints, like planning and sprint retrospectives.

---

01. Finite and Infinite Games. (2023, May 28). In Wikipedia.
https://en.wikipedia.org/wiki/Finite_and_Infinite_Games

The UX team has likely created countless wireframes and prototypes, conducted user research and discovery, documented the design system, and created component libraries.

These are valuable information resources just waiting to be uncovered. We all know we're supposed to review these things, but let's be honest: How often do you do it?

All this information will help explain why the team did the work the way it did so you know the best way to proceed. If you're joining a new team, this documentation is a gold mine of information to help you understand the players and rules. But even if you've been on the team for a while, it's never too late to dig into these things so you can start to play effectively.

Remember, though, that even though work is a game, the idea isn't to beat anyone. It's not to make anyone else lose. It's to keep playing as long as possible, which usually means you need your team to be successful, too. This way, we can all play together as long as possible.

Work should never be like Westeros, where we're trying to outsmart and stab our colleagues in the back. When I say game, this isn't what I'm talking about. So please don't turn work into a Game of Thrones.

Understand the players

We often talk about how there are no software standards across organizations. Why is that? Because those organizations are made up of people. And people are funny. They have their preferences, rituals, habits, and quirks.

Many of us are guilty of typecasting stakeholders, product managers, and engineers. But in reality, these people are all individuals. Treating one PM like the next is a recipe for disaster.

That's why it's so important to understand the individual people on our team. We need to get to know the stakeholders. We need to understand who makes decisions. Who answers to whom? What are their goals? What outcomes are they responsible for? How can they help us do our job? How can we help them to do their job better?

There are many ways to do this. If you're not remote, face-to-face meetings over coffee or walking around the block are no-brainers. If you're remote, this would be a video call–with the camera on!

These get-to-know calls are crucial to establishing a meaningful and mutually beneficial relationship. Don't focus entirely on work at first, anyway. Spend time getting to know the people you'll be working with as people first and foremost.

The next chapter will discuss the importance of building relationships and how to do that effectively with our team. I can't stress enough how important this is. We'll discuss the importance of 1:1s as a tool to nurture ongoing relationships, but 1:1s are just as crucial at the early stage as they are for teams that have been working together for years.

In these conversations with various team members, make sure you use the time to set proper expectations. What are their expectations for your role? What are their expectations for their role? Establish your expectations. This simple step is often overlooked, leading to a total misalignment and hurt feelings later. It's never too late to do this.

Talk about how you see yourself working with and supporting them in their role. Understand how they can help you and how you might help them in their day-to-day work.

If you're just joining a team and replacing someone who left, understand how they worked with the last person. How did it work out? Could something be improved? Given their understanding, ask who else might be worth meeting. Get a list of three to five people they think you'd be working with over time. Ask them for an introduction to build your credibility.

Your goal with these 1:1s is to get a sense of all the players you interact with throughout your day-to-day work, understand their internal network, and understand their motivations.

Will this person be an ally? Do you get a sense that they'd be a detractor? Would they back your work up when you hit a roadblock? Or do you get the sense you may need to apply extra attention to get them on your side?

Get a sense of who you'll work with best. There are likely people on your new team that you'll naturally gravitate towards. Then there are people you might butt heads with.

Foster those positive relationships and work to build up allies. You'll encounter many situations in your work where your team will disagree with your decisions. Or you won't have access to certain stakeholders but still need to influence them.

You're working to find someone on the team who can speak on your behalf when you're not around–Someone to be your advocate or sponsor. You'll use these allies and champions later when things get rough–And things will most definitely get rough.

If you're new to the team, you shouldn't push your priorities and opinions in these conversations. That time will come. It's OK to drop hints or provide opinions, but first, you must build relationships and trust before pushing your agenda.

Don't be afraid to ask stupid questions at any point here. Take advantage of being the "new person" and ask as many dumb questions as possible before you feel you can't ask them later. To be clear, you should never feel bad about asking stupid questions. But I know many will avoid asking "dumb questions." Consider this my permission to continue to ask silly questions long into your role. I won't judge you.

If someone uses a term or acronym you don't understand, ask them what it means. Write it down for reference later. You will run across many things like this as you have these conversations.

Take note of the language the team uses. If your team uses a specific vocabulary, acronyms, or buzzwords, adopt and use them too. This will help you sound less like an outsider and more like you're "one of them." Use in-group bias to your advantage, at least when starting.

I'd like to note that I'm not a fan of exclusive language, such as acronyms and buzzwords. But in this case, use the concepts of in-group bias to your advantage to help build trust early. Once you are well-established on the team, you may want to work to change these things. Just know that fighting this early on may not work to your advantage.

Your conversations with these players will give you insights into the rules. If you're just joining the team, this work will be critical to your success. But even if you've been on a team for a long time and found that you're hitting roadblock after roadblock, it might be beneficial to start doing these things now. It's never too late.

Understand the rules

Now that we understand all the players involved, we need to work to understand the rules.

The rules can be unofficial, like the words the team uses to describe something. They could also explain how the team works together. The rules could also be more official, like an established process, recurring meetings, who facilitates them, who is responsible for what, how decisions are made, how things are documented, etc. All of these could be examples of the rules.

Understanding all of these things is essential. If you're new to the team, it will help you when you're ready to start delivering work. You can transition into the day-to-day work without many hiccups or misunderstandings. But even if you've been on the team a while, these rules can help frame your conversations with your team as you go.

As you talk to your team they might mention these norms. But this is only one way to understand the rules. Another way to understand the rules is by reading documentation. Reading through page after page of documentation is likely not your idea of fun, but remember, documentation is a gold mine.

The team may have standard work documents or standard operation procedures (SOP), process maps of how things are done, documents on a shared drive, or onboarding videos. It's hard to say what teams will or won't have here–it could be almost anything and live almost anywhere.

If you're new, you will review this information extensively for the first few weeks before doing any actual work. If you have just never read through this before, you'll likely find the answers to some of your questions about why things are done a certain way. Some of these documents will take longer to read than others. Still, it's important to go through whatever information is available to you to understand the context around everything you'll eventually be responsible for.

You may find documentation about decision-making. If a team has done a retro, they may have documented it. You can look at past comments to see why certain decisions were made and why things are the way they are today.

You may find documentation about processes, such as how roadmaps are established, who decides what to build and why, or what stakeholders are included and why.

These examples are only a partial list. No matter how long you've been on the team, your team will have unique quirks worth you'll need to understand.

Understand what the company does. Why does it exist? How does it make money? Who is on the leadership team? Who is on the board? What do these people care about?

Understand the users and what their problems are as best you can. Read through all the personas, journey maps, service blueprints, empathy maps, and whatever artifacts the UX team has created over the years. Soak in as many maps, decks, videos, audio, notes, and anything available. If you can go through research decks, do that.

Get a sense of processes. How are projects kicked off? Who leads what activity? What regular activities do the teams have? What is your place in all of it?

Do your due diligence before asking questions. When you join a team, you'll have a million questions. But try to find the answer yourself before repeatedly asking a colleague. If you must ask, explain what you did to find the answer and how you couldn't. Then, ask the question. Try not to ping the same person every time. Try to spread the questions around if possible.

Now that you understand the rules, you will be better equipped to influence this group from the inside.

LET'S HEAR FROM THE EXPERTS

Dan Winer
Director of Product Design @ Kit

Dan shares his approach to joining a team by focusing on five key areas to understand the context, people, and operations.

When starting a new role, focus on five key areas to get up to speed: Colleagues, customers, the product, the business, and systems and process.

Colleagues

I encourage you to explore two dimensions: people you report to and your peers. In the first few weeks, you want to understand:

- ✓ Your manager's expectations of you and your role
- ✓ Your peers' priorities and opportunities they see for you

Dig into topics like strengths, areas of support needed, things they enjoy or dislike, company culture, concerns, and working style. Building personal relationships, trust, and comfort with colleagues is essential.

Customers

Understand who your customers are, why they come to you, and what problem you solve for them. It's the underlying context for why the company exists and what you're all doing.

Sometimes, getting on a customer call in your first few weeks at a company is hard. If you can't talk directly to customers, talk to colleagues who are in direct contact with them daily. In my opinion, support and CX teams are some of the best sources of customer insights. You may find a lot of value from watching sales calls, reading reviews, and looking through support chats.

The product

Dedicate plenty of time to going through the product as if you're a real customer. Add thoughts and questions to a big whiteboard of screenshots and annotations. This helps capture that beginner mindset and identify areas for improvement.

When considering the product, don't just evaluating the user experience; Also compile a list of questions relating to user behavior data that you want to investigate for more context.

The business

Learn how the business makes money, including pricing plans, pricing models, how deals are closed, the revenue streams, retention rates, and profitability. Map out the value streams to understand the company's relationships with partners, affiliates, and external vendors.

Systems and process

There are two priorities here: understand the current systems and processes and where you fit in, and using your fresh perspective, identify potential optimizations. Try not to rush into opinions on how things should be done; instead, ask about previous attempts and understand what has worked or not.

Understand how ideas and customer problems end up in the hands of designers. What path do they take? How collaborative is the process? What rituals and ceremonies are involved?

Learn about the design rituals and systems that ensure standards. Are there formal critiques? Do designers engage with users? How often does validation occur? What's the process for following up on designs in production? Focus on discovery and understanding what drives the company's success.

By focusing on these five areas, you can quickly get up to speed in a new role and make a meaningful impact.

Don't push your agenda too early

Early in my career, I had a bad case of naive idealism. I saw a problem, and I wanted to fix it. No one could stand in my way, so I told everyone there was a problem and wanted it fixed.

I didn't understand the context or the team's capabilities, so I couldn't provide the proper solution to the problem.

You can guess how often I could change anything–Not very often. This naive idealism did me no favors.

When you join a new team, the most important thing you can do in your first 30 days is to understand the players and rules before you attempt to change anything. Work to understand your place in the mess. Build empathy for your team. Try to understand where they're coming from and why they made their decisions.

As you complete this onboarding, you will undoubtedly have many ideas for improving things. However, understanding the rules is vital before bending or breaking them.

If you look at the outcomes we established prior in our example, we didn't set any outcomes related to change. Even if you've been explicitly hired to change things, it's essential to understand the larger context first.

At the end of these 30 days, our goal is to understand enough to speak coherently in a conversation. We want to understand context so that when you are ready give your opinion or suggest a change you will do it with the correct assumptions and context.

Remember that no one expects you to come out hitting grand slams on day one of your new role–to continue this game analogy. Making big decisions, designing amazing UIs, and influencing leadership, these things happen over time. Don't feel like anyone expects this from you right from your first day.

Focus on getting up to speed before trying to do any actual work.

Maximizing your first 30 days

Try to avoid having any preconceived notions and avoid making any assumptions early on. Things are usually the way they are for any number of reasons. It may be a terrible reason, but there was likely a reason.

Nothing builds trust better than shared experiences–Specifically complex or challenging experiences. If you see things needing change, experience the pain with the team before working to change anything. Once you experience that painful process, you'll have had the opportunity to talk about it with first-hand experience of why it was terrible. The team would have gone through it with you, and you'd be able to articulate what is broken and how it affected you personally. When you explain your new improvement, you'll have the credibility to back it up.

Wait to give your opinion until you feel like you have the pieces in place. Someone might ask you for your opinion early, and that is fine. But what you want to avoid is coming in hot, shaking things up before anyone is ready to do anything with your new ideas.

It's critical to be flexible. Use the team's shared language, work within the team's framework, and follow the status quo until you feel the team is open to change.

Practice pragmatism and understand what is possible and what is not. Remember that an infinite game goes on forever. If you see something you want to change, remember that institutional change often takes time, regardless of team size. This is a marathon, not a sprint.

Now, when you join a new time you'll go in with a plan. When you're ready to start shaking things up, you'll do it from a place of trusted authority.

Context is king

It doesn't matter if you're starting a new team or have been with the same organization for years. Context will help you make more informed decisions that resonate with users and align with business outcomes. Understanding the larger context isn't just a nice to have—it's a vital tool in our toolkit that shapes every design decision we make.

Context gives us the background we need to make smart decisions. Without it, we're simply guessing or giving subjective opinions. Context helps us avoid potential problems when dealing with our team members later. When we have a clear view of what affects our team's work, we can see potential issues before they happen and work to mitigate those problems early.

Most importantly, context helps us communicate more effectively. A shared understanding helps us better influence decisions and reduce misunderstandings and conflicts. Ultimately, context helps us to create a shared vision that makes it easier for us to move forward in the right direction, faster.

In the end, having the proper context is crucial to being an effective UX professional. It supports every decision, from the initial idea to final designs, ensuring our products are user-centered and strategically aligned. By understanding the larger context we work within, we can improve experiences, mitigate risks, and increase our influence. Embracing the larger context as a critical part of the design process will lead to smarter decisions and, ultimately, more successful products.

Chapter 03

Building Great Software with Great Relationships

What's more important than designing great products?

No, it's not winning fancy design awards. It is not getting the most followers online, and it's definitely not crafting a portfolio that is the envy of your designer friends.

No, what's more important than designing great products is delivering great products.

But we make it much harder to build great products when we're rigid and inflexible and when we're one of those designers everyone hates working with.

So, what's the secret to building great products?

The answer is *great relationships*.

H ere's the thing about software. It's generally pretty straightforward. You type the correct string of characters in your code editor of choice, assuming you typed it all in correctly, assuming you referenced all the proper functions, and assuming there are no typos, you should get functioning software. *In theory, anyway.*

Let's be clear: writing code is not a walk in the park. It's a complex process that requires attention to detail and a deep understanding of the system. But, in essence, it's a straightforward task.

Sure, knowing what to type in the first place is hard, but once you figure that out, software is *generally straightforward.*

So, if writing code is so straightforward, why is building great software so hard? The answer lies in the people.

Many engineers might disagree with my assessment, but I'm willing to wager that most engineers would agree with this point: *The other people on our team make the already difficult job of shipping great software even more difficult.*

You, me, the other designers, the PMs, the engineers, the stakeholders, all the processes we've created, and the red tape and bureaucracy we've set up make building great software hard.

We all have to deal with different and sometimes clashing personalities, conflicting opinions, past experiences that influence our perspectives, and the baggage we all carry.

This is what makes building great software hard. It has nothing to do with placing a single pixel in Figma, writing a single line of code in Visual Studio, or writing a single ticket in Jira.

Is there even a point in trying? There's always a point in trying!

I firmly believe that to break through this mess, you must have solid and meaningful relationships with your team because you simply can't build great software without great relationships.

There's just no way around it.

Great relationships make our life easier

Let me ask some questions:

- ✕ Are you constantly fighting with your dev or product teams?
- ✕ Are you getting left out of meaningful conversations?
- ✕ Are you getting the sense that your team doesn't trust you?

If you said yes to any of these, there's a good chance your relationship with your team isn't all that great. And if it's not all that great, you probably already know what that means.

This book has a central theme, and you've already heard me repeatedly say it: You can't build great software without great relationships. This message cannot be overstated.

I'm talking about relationships beyond your core design or UX team. If we want to ship great software, it's critical that we build great relationships with all the non-designers we work with.

- ✓ Relationships with stakeholders
- ✓ Relationships with product partners
- ✓ Relationships with engineering partners.
- ✓ Relationships with a core set of users.

Chapter 1 discussed a trait that makes a genuinely effective UX professional: Emotional Intelligence. Use your high emotional intelligence to apply empathy for your team before you even start thinking about a user. These core traits we addressed previously will help you build great relationships, and these relationships are critical to the entire team's success. Understanding and empathizing with your team members will foster a sense of connection and mutual respect, making the team dynamics smoother and more productive.

You're not the only one on the team. *Everyone's contribution is crucial*. Your relationship with your team members directly impacts the team's ability to deliver great software.

Whether product teams help move the process along, scrum masters remove blockers for engineers, or engineers type all that magical code, we need them—all of them.

When you start building meaningful relationships, you'll realize that those "difficult" people, who might be perceived as such due to their strong opinions or different working styles, aren't so tricky. They might be the key to unlocking your team's potential.

A relationship allegory

Meet our user, Jan. Jan, has a debilitating disease and uses two different apps to track her condition. She just wants a product that's easy to use because of all the stress she's already under.

Meet our first designer, Fred. Fred designs healthcare software. He designs one of Jan's daily apps to track her condition. He is a highly talented designer.

Fred is passionate about design. Unfortunately, he thinks he has all the answers and ensures everyone on his team knows he has all the answers. He generally doesn't like it when other people give input.

Unfortunately for Fred's team, he is challenging to work with.

Meet our second designer, Aimee. Aimee also designs healthcare software. Aimee designed one of the other apps Jan uses to track her condition. She is also a talented designer.

Aimee is passionate about design but knows she doesn't have

all the answers, so she encourages collaboration. Aimee's team loves working with her, and she gets along well with her team. By valuing and encouraging the input of her team members, Aimee fosters a sense of involvement and value, making her team more cohesive and productive.

Fred constantly butts heads with his coworkers. They've started leaving him out of meaningful conversations because they always end in a fight, and they're tired. Fred's team has stopped asking for his input because they think Fred is a jerk.

Fred has brilliant ideas for new features, but he can't seem to ship these valuable features. It appears Fred is losing his seat at the table.

On the other hand, Aimee makes it easy for her coworkers to work with her. They always include her in crucial conversations and get her opinion before they start.

Aimee has some brilliant ideas, and her team is happy to listen. Because of this, Aimee's team is shipping valuable features. Aimee's team thinks she's great, and they're glad she has that coveted seat at the table.

Same Hard Skills. Different Soft Skills

Fred and Aimee are talented designers, but Fred always seems to be left out of meaningful conversations. Fred can't influence his team and has had minimal impact on the final product.

On the other hand, Aimee has no problem influencing her team and has a much more significant impact on the final product.

What made Fred and Aimee so different?

Fred fostered apathy. Fred didn't want to waste time with regular check-ins. He didn't like small talk. He jumped right into meetings. In other people's meetings, he didn't pay attention and multitasked. Fred didn't bother learning about his teammates.

Aimee fostered empathy. Aimee had regular 1:1s with her team members. She didn't skip the small talk at the beginning of meetings or in the break room. She paid attention to what her team said and made them feel heard. She got to know her team on a personal level.

Fred fostered division. He thought he had all the answers, always shot down ideas from the rest of the team, and took all the credit for himself. Fred didn't play very well with others.

Aimee fostered collaboration. She knew she didn't have all the answers, but she was always happy to listen to other people's ideas. She didn't lead with "no." She always made sure to share credit with others on her team. Aimee was a real team player.

Fred fostered silence. When he answered questions, he talked in circles. He used industry terms and acronyms his team didn't understand. He spoke over everyone in meetings. Fred hated it when people came to him with concerns. Fred was a know-it-all.

Aimee fostered communication. She was clear and concise when answering questions. She didn't use buzzwords and acronyms to sound smart. She asked questions, and she listened. Aimee had an open-door policy and invited everyone on the team to reach out if they had concerns.

Fred fostered stagnation. Fred would get furious when his team didn't see his point of view. Fred liked his processes and didn't want to change. He was rigid and inflexible. He passed spec sheets over the fence and fought everyone on pixel perfection. Fred couldn't see the bigger picture.

Aimee fostered agility. Aimee knew she couldn't always convince her team, so she picked her battles. She was willing to change her process if someone had a better way. She worked closely with her engineering and product partners. Aimee didn't let perfection get in the way of the best her team could do.

Fred fostered doubt. Fred delivered work on his time and took on work he couldn't finish. He gave unrealistic timelines and shifted the blame when things didn't go right. Fred's team couldn't count on him.

Aimee fostered trust. She set the right expectations and delivered what she said she would when she said she would have it. She didn't overcommit to things she couldn't realistically complete. She took responsibility when things didn't go as planned. Aimee had integrity.

Fred fostered ignorance. He worked alone and refused to include anyone else on the team. He kept his findings to himself and didn't like to share. Fred siloed UX, so no one on his team knew what he was doing. They often questioned his contributions.

Aimee fostered UX literacy. Aimee didn't work in a silo. She included the right people in UX activities so they understood the complexity of her work. She constantly shared her findings with the larger team. Aimee showed the value of a good UX team.

Jan just wants software that works

The product Fred's team is building seems to have many usability issues, and she's simply not happy with the experience.

Jan is suffering because Fred and his team don't get along.

Aimee's product seems to work as expected, and she's pleased with her experience.

Jan is better off because Aimee and her team work well together.

This example is a very basic and overly exaggerated allegory. Nothing in software is black and white; many things go into delivering great software. It's true that how we choose to show up is not the only variable.

But the fundamental truth remains. Teams that work hard to build trust are higher performers. End users receive higher-quality products they want to use, which is ultimately good for the business's bottom line.

It's a win-win.

The benefits of great relationships

As simple as this allegory is, it touched on some of the significant benefits of ensuring we build great relationships with our teams.

One of the most essential benefits of fostering great relationships with our team, as Aimee did, is the trust that it promotes. Trust is the foundation of every good relationship, and it opens up nearly every benefit we see from high-performing teams.

When we build trust, we become partners. When we work to foster trust, the horror stories we hear other UX professionals talk about become less of a problem.

Our teams tend to include us earlier and often. We get included in the big-picture discussions, learn about constraints and goals early on, have more time to do the job right, and have an opportunity to influence early and often.

Being included earlier helps us build a shared understanding sooner, helps influence decisions sooner, and gets that seat at the table we're always asking for.

But first, we must look inward and ensure the problem isn't us. How we show up has an outsized impact on how our team perceives us and chooses to work with us.

Unfortunately, life is not always as simple as the allegory of Fred and Aimee. Some of us do everything Aimee did but can't deliver great products because we work with a team of Freds.

Before we look outward, I think it's essential to look inward and ensure the problem doesn't start with us.

As discussed in *Chapter* 3, there's a chance you'll end up with teams that don't function like you'd expect them to. That's normal, and we'll dig into some things you can do when we discuss design maturity in *Chapter* 6.

Building great relationships

Now that we've established how critical great relationships are, it's finally time to review some relationship-building tactics that have worked well for me over the years. As we go through these, note that every team is different: Every team will have different personalities, each team will operate with its unique rhythm, every relationship will have a different dynamic, and every situation will have a different context.

Get to know your team

I had been working on a relatively large software team for several years. I knew the product well and got along great with my regular team. But one day, my boss asked me to help with a new side project that was spinning up with a product manager I had never directly worked with before.

If you're not the only one on the team, you need *everyone* on the team.

The new product manager was brilliant, but she had a reputation for being somewhat tricky to work with. From the start, it felt like we were talking past each other, and we didn't seem to agree on much of anything. It was a struggle.

After one exceptionally tense meeting, it hit me. I don't know this person at all. I didn't understand how she communicated, and I didn't understand how to communicate with her.

The following week, I set up a weekly sync where we talked and got to know each other. The following weeks were like night and day–a complete reversal.

After that, I realized it was all about relationships–or, in my case, the lack of a relationship.

One of the most important things you can do is get to know the people on your team. However, we often put up walls or barriers in larger groups. We tend to open up more in smaller settings, which is why I like 1:1s so much.

1:1s are not just optional meetings, they are where the seeds of great relationships are planted. 1:1s provide a platform to discuss things beyond work, to understand your teammates on a personal level. These meetings are where you can truly connect and build a strong bond with your team members individually.

If you don't already have regular 1:1s set up, schedule one with key team members. Schedule a short meeting every other week. I like to do 25 minutes so you don't take up half an hour. This sub-30-minute timing shows your team that you respect them and their time.

Small talk is vital for laying the foundations of a great relationship. It may seem like a time-waster at work, but it's a powerful tool for building connections and understanding your team members personally.

In these meetings, don't avoid the small talk

If you struggle with small talk, don't miss Tim Yeo's advice on making small talk easier on *page* 74. Tim shares a simple framework for small talk in his book, *The Quiet Achiever.* [01]

Talk a little about yourself. But ask your colleagues questions. Don't spend most of the time talking about yourself. Let them speak for the majority of the time. Find something in common to connect with them. Do you both like board games? Do you both like basketball? Do you have a favorite hobby in common? For instance, you could ask about their favorite board game or the last game they played. Or if they like basketball, you could ask about their favorite team or player. These are just a few examples of initiating a conversation and finding common ground.

If they talk about their kids, partners, or dogs, take notes, as we discussed in *Chapter* 2. These things make small talk much more effortless later and keep those relationships going.

Use the time in these meetings to set expectations

At work, many conflicts stem from misaligned expectations. As we discussed in *Chapter* 2, setting expectations early is key. Setting clear expectations is never too late, even if you've been working with the team for a while. This proactive approach can help you navigate conflicts and maintain a smooth relationship.

If you've been working with this person for a while and there has been some tension, there's a reasonable chance expectations are off. It might be an excellent opportunity to clear the air when you have them alone. If you haven't done it yet, now is a fantastic time to discuss your expectations for the other person.

---

01. https://www.thequietachievr.com/

If you're in person, leave the office and go for a walk to get some coffee down the block. Make this enjoyable and comfortable for both of you.

Chapter 4 underscored the importance of 1:1s when joining a new team. These meetings are not just for introductions but also for building relationships with your team on an ongoing basis. All the tips we discussed previously apply here. Remember, 1:1s are not just a one-time thing but a valuable tool throughout your career, so make sure to give them the attention they deserve!

Embrace diverse cultures

One distinct advantage of working for a large, multi-national corporation is exposure to diverse cultures. This exposure is a fantastic opportunity, as it can lead to a richer, more innovative team dynamic. However, a culture clash can cause headaches and problems for the software team.

Several years back, I was fortunate to travel to Budapest to meet with our new 50-plus-person team of engineers, PMs, and UX designers. I spent the entire 8-hour flight practicing introducing myself in Hungarian.

"Hagy vagy? Jeremy vagyok"

It was about as badly pronounced and awkward as you'd expect. My Southern-Louisiana-Hungarian accent got me a lot of laughs, but years later, I still had people talking about how much the team appreciated the effort.

If you're fortunate enough to work with international teams, learning a few words in their language goes a long way. You don't have to be fluent, but remembering just a few key phrases like "good morning," "How are you," and "I'm sorry" will be much appreciated. You may be surprised how few people, especially

Americans, even attempt to make such a small gesture as this. This appreciation is especially true if the language is perceived as complex.

Your team will appreciate that you're learning their language.

Learn some of their customs and their holidays. Put the holidays on your calendar so you know when they are, and wish them a happy holiday when they come around. Remember not to bug them when they're off, but you're stuck at work on the other side of the world. Also, be mindful of cultural norms and practices. For example, in some cultures, it's disrespectful to address someone by their first name without their permission. Understanding and respecting these differences will show your colleagues that you value their culture and their comfort.

Most importantly, be aware of time zones. Don't message them at night, their time, while you're still at work. Those notifications can get frustrating quickly.

These small gestures will go a long way to improve your relationships with colleagues abroad.

Great relationships need nurturing

The people we work with are humans—yes, the product managers, stakeholders, and engineers too! The relationships we build at work are not much different from those we make with friends and acquaintances outside of work. Empathy, the ability to understand and share the feelings of others, is a crucial element in building and nurturing these relationships. It allows us to connect with our colleagues deeper, fostering a sense of understanding and connection.

Like any meaningful relationship, those at work don't suddenly become significant overnight. Relationships take time and effort

LET'S HEAR FROM THE EXPERTS

Christopher Nguyen
Founder UX Playbook

Chris shares insights about how effective 1:1s can make you a more engaged employee and accelerate your career growth.

As an employee, 1:1 meetings with your manager can be a powerful tool for personal growth, career development, and open communication. These regular check-ins provide a valuable opportunity to discuss your progress, voice concerns, and align your goals with the company's objectives.

Embrace the fact that this time is primarily for you. Your manager has set aside this time to focus on your needs, concerns, and aspirations. It's your chance to drive the conversation and shape your professional journey.

Typically scheduled weekly or bi-weekly for 30-60 minutes, consistency is key. While it's okay to occasionally cancel if there's truly nothing to discuss, be cautious about making this a habit.

To get the most out of your 1:1s consider these best practices:

- ☐ **Be punctual:** Show respect for your manager's time and commitment to the process.

- ☐ **Come prepared:** Maintain a shared document for topics, questions, or concerns.

- ☐ **Own the agenda:** Prioritize topics that matter most to you.

- ☐ **Be open to change:** Occasionally suggest a change of scenery for more relaxed conversations.

Consider including these topics:

While the specific agenda may vary, consider these topics:

- ☐ **Progress updates**: Share achievements and challenges.
- ☐ **Career development**: Discuss long-term aspirations and growth opportunities.
- ☐ **Feedback**: Both give and receive constructive feedback.
- ☐ **Work-life balance**: Address any workload or personal issues affecting your work.
- ☐ **Company insights**: Gain understanding of the company's direction and your role's contribution.

Making the Most of Your Time

Ensure productive 1:1s with these strategies:

- ✓ **Be honest and transparent**: Embrace open dialogue.
- ✓ **Ask questions**: Seek clarification on goals or expectations.
- ✓ **Propose solutions**: Come prepared with ideas to improve.
- ✓ **Follow up**: Take notes and act on commitments made.
- ✓ **Reflect**: Evaluate each meeting to improve future sessions.

Remember, effective 1:1s are a two-way street. While your manager facilitates these meetings, you play a crucial role in making them valuable. By actively participating and driving the conversation, you can turn these regular check-ins into powerful tools for your professional growth and job satisfaction.

Embrace this opportunity to build a stronger relationship with your manager, align your goals with the company's vision, and take charge of your career development. With the right approach, 1:1s can become a highlight of your work week, propelling you towards success in your current role and beyond.

to grow and blossom into something more, so be patient and consistent in your efforts.

Building great relationships isn't a one-time thing. Once you've built them, you need to nurture them over time.

I always liked to make a point to get lunch with someone from my team at least once a month. A former supervisor let us use our corporate cards to expense the meal to get to know our stakeholders and product partners. It never hurts to ask if you can do this, too.

In an interview with Kate Pincott,[02] she talked about how she sets reminders to reach out to people she hasn't spoken to in a while with a joke or an interesting story. She's always looking for excuses to reach out to people she hasn't spoken to recently.

And really, you don't need an excuse. Everyone loves a quick email check-in to see how they are doing!

It may sound forced or inauthentic initially, but remember to consider it more of an intentional act when forming long-term relationships with your team.

Remote teams

I'm no advocate for returning to the office nine to five, five days a week, but I felt I lost something going fully remote. After working remotely post-COVID, I drifted apart from the people I saw and spoke to daily. I realized that if I wasn't working with them daily, we could sometimes go months or more without speaking.

One of the hardest things I've found about working remotely is losing that sideline talk—the chat over the coffee machine, in the break room, or at the water cooler—all of those random conversations you might drop in on when you're at the office.

02. https://www.beyonduxdesign.com/episode/90-the-art-of-perspective-mastering-the-reframe-with-kate-pincott

If you're remote, these side conversations need to be intentional.

If you have a team active on a tool like Slack or Discord, they may have different channels for different interests. At a previous job, we had all kinds of channels, from DIY to landscaping, music to dogs, fishing, and bikes. We even have a Slack channel where people would talk about fast food.

If your team doesn't have these things, why not create them and encourage the rest of your team to join these channels?

Many people tend to overlook the importance of small talk. I've mainly seen this firsthand after many teams went fully remote post-COVID. When meetings start, many of us will stay quiet for the first minute or two until the meeting officially begins. Sometimes, others will insist on getting to business right at the start of the meeting.

I suggest you avoid doing that. Take advantage of the few minutes this group is together. Use the small window to ask how people are doing. If it's earlier in the week, ask how their weekend was. If it's later in the week, ask if they have any big plans for the weekend. You might ask how their kids are doing if you know their kid was sick. Or if their dog was in the vet, you can ask how the pup is holding up. These seemingly insignificant side conversations are critical.

Many of us are so worried about looking like we're working hard that we miss the long-term productivity boost of getting along with our team. Remember that we miss opportunities to build stronger team bonds when we don't do these things.

Of course, sometimes people are busy or short on time. So, read the room and know when it might make sense to skip small talk.

Another good relationship-building opportunity is scheduling regular 1:1s with key team members. These 1:1s don't have to be every week. Everyone is different. It could be once a month. You'll know the right rhythm. Just keep it consistent, and remember to keep these meetings fun. Remember to save some time in these meetings to talk about something outside of work to get to know them better and nurture those relationships.

Go to these meetings with the mindset that you can help them solve a problem. Ask if you can do anything to help them. This mindset will go a long way to building their trust and empathy.

Don't force it. You need to be genuine to build genuine relationships with your team. The point of all this is to build empathy for your team so you can better understand what they need later and how you can best help them when the time comes.

Build empathy for your team

Earlier in the chapter, I discussed a project I had been asked to help out work on with a particularly "difficult" product manager. At first, we didn't get along, but after a few coffee runs and a handful of 1:1s, I understood her a bit more, and we started working well together.

In this case, I came into our meetings thinking only about myself and what the UX team needed to do. What I was forgetting was trying to understand her perspective, what was important to her, and, critically, how she communicated these things. Once I started to truly listen, our relationship completely changed for the better.

As UX professionals, we talk about empathy for users all the time. But what I don't hear often enough is the need to have empathy for our team. Having empathy for our team is no less critical.

In fact, it may be *more* significant.

Too often, I see UX teams falling into the trap of "othering" those outside the UX team. It frequently ends up being the UX designer vs a developer, UX designer vs product manager, or UX designer vs stakeholder.

To be fair, there are standoffish engineers and lousy product managers, but they are not the norm.

More often than not, when we struggle with cross-functional collaboration, it's because the effort wasn't made (on either side) to understand where the other is coming from. Pushy PM? Short Engineer? There could be any number of things going on—both inside and outside of work—that you might not be aware of.

There are, no doubt, things that are stressing them out. There may be constraints that we weren't aware of. There are likely outside pressures they may be feeling from their boss or other teams. You just won't know unless you make an effort to find out.

Have an open-door policy

What does an "open door policy" look like? Does it mean you treat your extended team like a new intern? Not at all. What this looks like for you and your team might be different from what has worked for me, so don't be afraid to adjust to suit your needs.

I always include engineers, product managers, and stakeholders in early co-design sessions. Stakeholders and product managers always enjoy participating in the process. It always depends on the engineer. Some wanted to attend, others didn't, but all appreciated the invite. It makes them feel like they have a hand in crafting features and helps build buy-in early.

When I do these types of things, I get much less pushback from my team later. There are several reasons for this.

It makes the product manager's job easier because they can document features early and ensure that what we're working on aligns with their roadmaps, even if they aren't widely shared yet.

Engineers enjoy being involved early and having the opportunity to influence technology, such as components or third-party services. Being involved early reduces their stress and gives them more time to think about requirements and how to work around complex or difficult constraints.

It's a mutually beneficial experience for everyone involved. It tends to alleviate many of the typical back-and-forth conversations and accompanying stress that accompany a more traditional "design handoff."

Lastly, it's essential to be present simply. It's important to be available to answer questions and work through challenges and obstacles. That looks like attending scrum ceremonies when I can or having someone from my team available during planning or refinement to help answer questions. I've found that these things make everyone's job more effortless in the long run.

In *Chapter 1*, we established what UX is: the experience a user has. Everyone should feel like they own some aspect of this experience. Let them in and help build their empathy for users.

To be trusted partners and foster collaboration, we need to walk the walk. We need an open-door policy that brings our team with us along the way.

If the design maturity of our team is low, it likely isn't because the people on the team hate the UX team or the users. It's most likely because they don't know the alternatives. Like it or not, part of our job is to help get them there and build UX literacy on the team. So how do we do that? We include them!

Include your important product and engineering partners in brainstorming, whiteboard, or co-design sessions. Get them involved with planning research. Take them along when you do research trips so they can see the effort put into planning, execution, and synthesis. Show them that it's not all gut instincts and coloring with crayons.

Include your team in usability study sessions as note-takers or observers. Include your team in design critiques so they can see the logic behind design decisions.

Let them see the process and the science behind what we do so they don't think we're just drawing pretty pictures all day. Show them we're not just pushing pixels; our input is valuable.

Many on your team would be thrilled to tag along. I suggest you allow these people to peek behind the curtain, especially if they're curious. However, remember that not everyone on your team will be excited to participate. Don't force them or, even worse, have them do the actual work of the UX team.

Being present early and often will elevate the UX team as trusted experts and partners. Your availability will go a long way towards improving your relationships with your team and how your team looks to work with you and the rest of the UX team in the future.

Let your team in and see those relationships blossom.

Simplify Your Work With Internal Networking

You've built strong relationships with your core team. But how well do you know the rest of the people in your larger organization?

Can you name five or ten people outside of your direct team? Do you know what they do? Do you know why they're assigned to the things they're assigned to? Do you know how it impacts you and your team?

If you stopped networking the minute you accepted an offer, you're likely missing out on all the context and career growth opportunities.

I grew up in New Orleans, where who you know is often more important than what you know. This certainly isn't always good, but it taught me valuable lessons.

My dad worked for GMAC, the finance arm of General Motors, his entire career—straight out of the Marine Corps, fresh off a tour in Vietnam, until the day he retired. When I graduated high school, he told me something that has stuck with me my entire career: "Son," he said, sounding more like a Marine Corps Drill sergeant than a loving dad, "If you want to get anything done, you take someone to lunch."

Two decades later, even with the work-from-home revolution, the essence of his advice holds. The medium may have changed, but the idea remains the same: Whether over a hot cup of coffee or a video call, personal interactions with your colleagues are often the key to getting things done.

I know a lot of people dread networking. The idea of going to some silly event after work is the last thing they want to do. But networking is more than showing up to a bar, slapping on a nametag, and shuffling around for 45 minutes before leaving.

Lots of people look at networking as a necessary evil. Something they dread doing. Something they think only kissasses and brown nosers do. Some people think networking seems forced or fake. Some people feel like they're just bugging people or bothering them. But I'd argue if you're doing that, what you're doing isn't networking!

Understanding why we network gives us a professional incentive to get out there and get to know more people, especially after landing the job.

There are several reasons to continue networking internally after you land your next role. Some of them seem selfish at first. They may seem like you're playing into the political game. But it's all about your motivations. If you're on the fence about continuing to network internally, I would encourage you to consider the benefits of continuing this networking.

The benefits of internal networking

Here are a few key benefits to networking internally that I have experienced firsthand:

- ✓ It helps build your social capital
- ✓ Insights from other teams add context
- ✓ Cross-functional collaboration becomes easier
- ✓ It makes everyone's job easier
- ✓ It helps find a mentor
- ✓ It helps with career growth
- ✓ It opens opportunities we wouldn't have found otherwise

I'm sure others might have different personal experiences with internal networking; these were just a few of mine.

Build Your Social Capital

There's something to be said when you're on a first-name basis with the CIO and top-tier executives of a Fortune 500 company. When this CIO has your phone number and texts you about new software concepts they read about recently because it reminded them of you, you know you're doing something right.

Some might call this "personal brand." Unfortunately, I've seen enough people deride personal brand as a negative lately that I think it might be time for it to get a rebrand.

So, instead of thinking of this as your personal brand, I like to think of this more as "social capital."

Not many professionals think about social capital until they start to move up in their careers, but by then, it's often too late. Thinking about this now will put you far ahead of your peers when it comes to career growth later.

McKinsey & Company, one of the big global business consulting agencies, defines social capital as "the presence of networks, relationships, shared norms, and trust among individuals, teams, and business leaders." [01]

An excellent way to think about it is it's the glue that holds organizations together. It's the people you know inside the company. It's the team's culture and the language your team uses. It's the players and the rules we talked about in *Chapter* 2.

Your social capital is your standing within that ecosystem. It's how well you are known within your team. The more social capital you have, the better off you are.

So far, we've covered a lot about relationships in this book. All of these things we have discussed about relationships are meant to help build not only your social capital but also the social capital of your team. Improving your social capital will help everyone improve their performance and effectiveness in the long run.

Insights from other teams add context

Because you're networking and increasing your visibility across teams, this leads directly to improved clarity into what those other teams are doing. Early insights from other teams provide a strategic advantage, allowing you to make more informed decisions and contribute more effectively to your team.

---

01. Lauricella, T., Parsons, J., Schaninger, B., & Weddle, B. (2022, August 2). Network effects: How to re-build Social Capital and improve corporate performance. McKinsey & Company. https://www.mckinsey.com/capabilities/people-and-organizational-performance/our-insights/network-effects-how-to-re-build-social-capital-and-improve-corporate-performance

For instance, understanding the marketing team's strategies can help you design a product that aligns with their campaigns, or knowing the challenges faced by the sales team can guide your solutions to address those issues.

Your contribution to these cross-functional collaborations is vital and can make a significant difference.

As a UX professional, I hope one thing has become clear from my ranting and raving up until now. For software teams, solving the correct problems at the right time in the right way is our number one priority. And you can't solve the correct problems at the right time in the right way without the proper context.

And where do you get the proper context? The right context comes from conversations with people outside our core team who aren't directly involved with our products. This is especially true in large matrixed organizations, where employees often report to multiple managers or work across different departments, like corporate or in-house teams.

If our organization is large enough, the context can get muddier and muddier the more we are removed from big-picture conversations happening at the top. Designing our software in a silo doesn't help the larger organization in the long run, and it doesn't benefit users or the business in any meaningful way.

For our team to be successful, we have to understand the problems the business is trying to solve, not just the issues a set of users has. These things would be aligned in a perfect world, but that isn't always the case. We must consider the constraints as much as user needs as we do our day-to-day work.

So, using your social capital to gain insights and context about those business priorities and overall constraints is a massive advantage of networking internally.

Cross-functional collaboration becomes more manageable

Imagine you've been tasked with helping the sales team decrease contract turnaround time by the end of the quarter to meet their sales targets. So, you have a sales team counting on you to deliver a product to help them work more efficiently.

Suppose you don't know anyone outside of your core team well. In that case, you might proceed with what you think is correct: starting with user interviews, mapping out processes, conducting usability studies, creating prototypes, and preparing everything for engineering.

While this approach may work, it carries significant risks if you don't consider the larger context. By working in a silo, not discussing anything with anyone outside your core team, you might discover too late that another team is working on something very similar. Worse yet, their project might have an executive sponsor prioritizing it over yours. Suddenly, you've wasted valuable time that could have been spent on something more impactful.

Another potential pitfall is overlooking critical data dependencies on source systems—systems the sales team might not even know exist because they see it all as one tool. These dependencies require involvement from other teams that can't accommodate last-minute requests, which could delay your tool's launch.

Your manager or stakeholders may not be aware of these dependencies, and you may not uncover them by conducting stakeholder and user interviews alone.

In both scenarios, a lack of networking means wasting time on unnecessary work that doesn't add value to the business or the users. If you had known about these issues beforehand, you could have focused on something more valuable.

Tim Yeo
Chief Introvert, The Quiet Achiever

Tim shares a simple framework for making small talk. Learn more in his book, The Quiet Achiever: www.thequietachievr.com/book

When it came to small talk, I seldom knew what to say or how much detail to share. Why would someone I just met ask me about my weekend? How interested were they? Why do people say things they do not mean?

Small talk is like a verbal handshake before the real conversation begins. Imagine extending your hand to shake and having the other person not notice or reciprocate. Awkward, isn't it? The same applies to small talk. When you do not engage in small talk, the other party feels like they have extended their hand, but you aren't shaking it back.

I had to learn how to make small talk, and you can use Maslow's hierarchy of needs as a framework. Maslow's hierarchy suggests people are motivated to fulfill basic needs before moving on to more advanced needs.

There are five levels: (Top) Self-actualization, esteem needs, love and belonging needs, safety needs, (Bottom) physiological needs. Start at the bottom and move up. Topics based on the lower levels have the widest applicability. We are all human, and these topics are our lowest common denominator.

The lower the level, the higher your chances of having something in common and making a connection. Remember: You do not need to be interesting, you just need to be relatable.

Your small talk topics can be positive or negative. Life is not always a bed of roses, and negative stories can make you relatable. For example:

Self-actualization: You were at a concert last night, but you wonder if that could have been your life too if you had picked a different path ("You know, I was in a rock band in high school...")

Esteem: You were the champion of the arcade game Space Invaders, but over the weekend, your partner beat your high score (and they do not even like Space Invaders!)

Love and belonging: Your favorite sports team, one you have supported for years, lost the championship over the weekend

Safety: Your landlord raised the rent again and you might have to move because you can no longer afford to live there

Physiological: You commuted to the office in the rain, so now you have wet socks and cold feet (nobody likes wet socks)

Small talk opens doors and possibilities. It has broadened the range of people I could connect with and helped me avoid countless awkward silences, making others feel comfortable working with me. Getting good at small talk allowed me to confidently connect with new people and deepen existing relationships. The more people I met, the wider my network grew, and the deeper the relationships I formed became.

Small talk is not real talk; that comes after. I suspect people neglect practicing and developing small talk because it seems trivial. The hard stuff is important, but do not underestimate the power of small talk. In the long run, learning to introduce yourself confidently and making small talk will help you have the most impact. It's a numbers game. Tiny habits, done well, accumulated over time.

These scenarios sound like an edge case but are common in large companies, especially those with large in-house teams. It's common for projects to spin up without the larger team's knowledge, with massive organizations developing products in their bubbles, guided more by departmental priorities and budgets than company-wide strategy.

This phenomenon is called Conway's Law,[02] and it suggests that teams often create systems that mirror their organizational structure rather than following a deliberate, thought-out plan. Sadly, this is a common occurrence—so common that it's got its own name!

It's also common to see communication break down and a need for more transparent documentation. This may lead to a reliance on "tribal knowledge" for design and architectural decisions. Certain team members become the sole repositories of unwritten insights and understanding.

However, there's an alternative scenario.

By engaging in internal networking, you can connect the dots sooner. You might discover early on that another team is already working on a similar project unknown to your stakeholders. You can facilitate communication between different teams to help deliver dependencies sooner or find workarounds for constraints earlier. This internal networking can make your tool available sooner, improving business outcomes and user experiences.

You might think, "Hey, I'm just a UX designer. That's not my job." And you'd be right - it may be your leader's job to connect these dots. But this is what an effective follower does. We'll introduce the concept of Followership and how being a more effective follower can help your career in *Chapter 8*.

---

02. https://martinfowler.com/bliki/ConwaysLaw.html

Effective followership in this context means taking the initiative to find the people and bridge gaps in communication or knowledge. You're going beyond your immediate job duties, like wireframes and user research, to identify opportunities and facilitate connections that benefit the entire organization.

In a perfect world, our leadership team and managers would have insights into these issues and highlight them early for us. Unfortunately, supervisors and middle managers are often far removed from these problems. Lower-level individual contributors can identify these issues more quickly because they're in the trenches, seeing things supervisors often miss.

Putting users first and embracing followership opens up our horizons in exciting ways. If we genuinely prioritize users, we'll work to solve their problems by doing things we wouldn't usually consider part of a UX professional's "job." Connecting dots is one of these things.

Once we gain situational awareness from networking, it becomes easier to implement our plans. More context helps us better execute with our partners and cross-functional teams. By broadening our perspective through internal networking, we position ourselves to deliver more impactful solutions and drive better outcomes for our users and the business.

It helps you find a mentor

I got lucky with my first job at a giant company. During my first week, I was assigned a buddy to help onboard me to the company. This buddy wasn't there to help me with my day-to-day work. Instead, their role was to help me get my computer set up, make sure I got my badge, get all my computer set up, and ensure I could access all the systems I needed to access.

What made me so lucky was that this buddy turned out to be a company veteran. She was starting her 16th year when I came on board. At the time, I didn't realize it, but those casual chats we had ended up saving me from a ton of headaches. She knew how to navigate all the corporate bureaucracy and red tape that I would've been fumbling with for who knows how long without her advice.

Many junior professionals overlook finding a mentor until later in their careers. While finding a mentor outside of work is helpful, finding an internal mentor can be a game-changer.

Finding this mentor early can help you in many ways. In addition to the traditional ways an external mentor can be helpful, an internal mentor can add a layer of context to their advice.

→ A good internal mentor will help you navigate the organization's politics.

→ A good internal mentor can be open and honest about how you're aligning with company priorities.

→ A good internal mentor can apply company-specific advice to help you grow your career faster.

If you're new to the company, an internal mentor is especially beneficial. If you find a mentor inside your company, they'll be able to give you more specific advice, like helping you navigate some of the unique quirks outsiders would never know about.

It opens internal job opportunities

When I mention that I spent eight years at the same company, people often assume I was stuck on one team, working on the same product the whole time. But that couldn't be further from the truth.

Insights from other teams provide a strategic advantage.

Networking and tapping into my social capital opened doors to many opportunities. I jumped on different stretch projects, explored new roles, and met many people without leaving the company. It was like having multiple jobs without all the headaches of job hunting.

The more you build your social capital, the more you improve your reputation at work. Your manager will start to think about you for promotions. Others might identify you for special projects or consider giving you more responsibility. It can have a natural snowball effect. This could mean more money and even more opportunities for future growth.

Networking internally might open up many internal opportunities you may otherwise never know about. Larger companies often post internal-only roles. No one outside the company will see them. These roles are not posted on public job boards, so you'll never find these roles by searching online.

Someone may have left, and a team in another org is looking to backfill that position. Or it might be a completely new position that needs to be filled. Finding someone who already works at the company reduces a lot of the time and effort required for onboarding–they already have a badge, they already have a computer, and they already understand the ins and outs of the company and how everything works. They can start contributing back almost immediately.

This kind of thing happens a lot.

Because you've built up your social capital, someone outside your team might think about you specifically for the role. Or you might hear about an opening by keeping your ear to the ground so you know to ask about it.

Either way, you likely wouldn't know about these opportunities unless you actively network and keep in touch with people outside your core team.

You can use networking to get a promotion or a raise without quitting and leaving the company altogether. Maybe you don't like working with your core team, or perhaps you don't like the project you're on. Finding an alternative internal role keeps you from quitting a company you might otherwise be pleased with.

Internal opportunities are a huge advantage of keeping these relationships strong, especially if you work for a larger company.

It helps with overall career growth

I worked closely with an executive who headed up Program Management for a few years at my company. We had a good working relationship, but like many things in the corporate world, he eventually left to pursue an external opportunity. I figured that was that, and life went on as usual.

A few years later, I got a random call. This same executive had landed a new role as CIO at another Fortune 500 company. He wanted to bring me on his team to help them with his planned digital transformation initiative.

It did not work out for various reasons, but it is a potent reminder that you never know when those old connections might resurface and lead to something significant in your career journey.

While your external network is undeniably beneficial for career growth, it's important to remember that the people you've built meaningful relationships with within your company may also move on. These connections could bring opportunities directly to you that you might not have discovered otherwise.

Proactively networking can steer your career growth in the desired direction. For instance, you might befriend a lead who later transitions to a manager or director role outside the company. You might also establish a connection with a director who later becomes a CIO at another company. These relationships could lead to future opportunities that align with your career goals, such as being recommended for a new role, being included in a high-profile project, or receiving mentorship from a senior leader.

Some of these opportunities may be things you may have never found on a random job board. The people you've worked with may have you in mind, and there's a good chance you won't be competing with many other people for the role if they thought about you specifically.

Internal networking tips

At this point, you may be thinking: "This all sounds great, but where do I start?!" Perhaps you've just started a new job and are already stressed with everything you must do to get up and running. Or maybe you've been at your company for a little while, but you just have no idea how to reach out to new people.

This can all be overwhelming, but let's look at some specific networking tips that can help you navigate these situations.

Start with your core team

The first thing you should do is start with the people you already know and work with every day. Start with your core team!

If you aren't already having regular 1:1s with your core team, now is a perfect time to start. 1:1s are not just for you and your manager. As we've stressed, 1:1s are an excellent opportunity to have informal chats with colleagues, keep your ear to the ground to connect the dots, and build situational awareness.

These 1:1s are undoubtedly good for networking, but this will also help you be more effective in your role. Refer back to *Chapter 3* for some more specific tips here.

Be strategic

Once you've established a rhythm with your core team, it's time to be strategic. Identify who else in the company you should know. Use your current network to ask around. Consider upstream or downstream dependencies and the tools your users use daily. If you're working on an internal software team, it would be a good idea to look at your users and the organization they work for and get to know them. Getting to know these people can broaden your network and potentially uncover new and valuable insights.

Most companies have an internal directory or org chart where you can look up teams and find people to contact.

When you do reach out, have a good reason for contacting them. You may want to know these people or their team more or want more information about their work because it might align with your current project. Let them know that you can help them. Connecting with them and sharing information may benefit them or their team. It could also be something else entirely.

Regardless, I like to send a DM using Slack or Teams. I tell them why I'm reaching out and ask if it's OK to set up an informal 25-minute chat. I don't want to take up too much of their time or the entire half an hour. I like to leave room for them to go to the bathroom or get a coffee before their next meeting. Even if they're not super busy, this shows that I respect their time.

From there, see how the conversation goes. If the work your teams are doing makes it a good idea to have regular check-ins, you could have them bi-weekly, monthly, quarterly, ad hoc, or whatever makes sense.

There's also the possibility of no connection or overlap at all, and regular check-ins don't make sense. Either way, you'll have an additional data point for the future. It may be helpful later if someone else asks about this team or their product. You'll have an answer.

Join affinity groups

Not every company has affinity groups, but many do. They are often more informal groups that co-workers have set up to connect employees with various interests who typically wouldn't work together. For instance, where I have worked in the past, we had an African American Forum, an LGBTQ+ ally group, a veterans group, an Asian-Pacific Alliance group, a parent network, and many more.

Joining affinity groups is a great way to start a conversation with people you may not have worked with before. These groups often provide a platform for sharing experiences, learning from others, and building relationships with colleagues from diverse backgrounds and departments. And in this case, what's great is they are likely outside your core team, giving you a broader perspective and potentially opening up new opportunities.

Ask who else you should meet

When you talk with people outside your core team towards the end of the call, ask who else they think you should know. You can say, "I'm interested in diving more into this process. Is there someone else you think I should talk to to get a different perspective?" Or "Is there someone else who might know more?" Or "Is there someone else's perspective I should get here?" They'll tell you exactly who to reach out to.

This can happen on the call, but if you run out of time, this can be a follow-up email.

If they're willing, asking for an introduction would be a good idea. Warm introductions make growing your network a lot easier. Remember, this will also help you and your team get work done in the future.

Try off-the-wall ideas

My co-host Derek from my show Retro Time // A Software Podcast and I worked together for a long time. We were part of an organization that had almost 1,000 people.

We noticed a problem and found a unique way to address it. Because the organization was so big, teams tended to work in silos. Knowing what 1,000 people were doing was impossible.

Because Derek and I were known around the office as "the two dudes with a podcast," we asked, "What if we do a podcast-style interview with random people on the team?" We could record the Teams meeting and post the video to Slack.

We called it "Makers on Teams Drinking Coffee."

Every month, we interviewed a random person from the team and asked them silly questions. We played a game with them and had them identify a random company acronym. It was a lot of fun and pretty entertaining if I say so myself.

Spoiler alert: no one got the acronyms right.

Not only did we meet these people we would have otherwise not met, but everyone on the team got to know them better, too.

Solving the *right problems* at the *right time* in the *right way* is our team's #1 priority.

Most importantly, it increased our social capital.

People started to watch these silly videos and looked forward to the next one. People began to talk about them, and word of mouth spread. People shared the idea with other orgs.

Our team felt more comfortable talking to us in meetings and wasn't afraid to reach out if they had issues. I'm convinced the connections we made helped us be more effective at our jobs.

The whole thing was silly, but it was a unique way to build our social capital with the larger 1,000-person organization and spread a little joy doing it. All by having a conversation and posting it on Slack.

There are other interesting things you can try. Think about your social capital and what you want to be known for. There may be some out-of-the-box ways to network that show off your unique personality and skills.

Networking for Introverts

These things have worked well for me, but I am no introvert.

I'm sure many people reading this have already had a nervous breakdown thinking about doing some of these things. So, I wanted to provide a few tips for introverts I've heard throughout the years because I don't want to leave anyone out.

First, let me be clear: Just because you're an introvert doesn't mean you can't do this.

The most important thing is to do what makes you comfortable. For instance, you may find virtual networking easier. Excellent, do that. That's probably the norm nowadays, anyway.

Remember that networking is more about asking questions, shutting up, and listening than anything else. You shouldn't be talking the whole time anyway. Most introverts are already pretty good listeners. So introverts, you have an advantage here!

Maybe you're not great at coming up with questions on the fly. That's fine! Have some notes handy to make sure you remember to ask specific questions during the conversation.

If the "Makers on Teams Drinking Coffee" idea is out of the question, maybe you can try something similar asynchronously. Try sending a list of questions to a colleague, create a blog post, and share that with your team.

This list is certainly not exhaustive, and I'm no expert on introverts, but a personal favorite is a series on networking for introverts that my friend Lex Roman did on her show, *Low Energy Leads*.[03] She interviewed several successful introverts on how they like to network. Make sure to check that out. I learned a lot tuning in.

This chapter's expert, Tim Yeo, offers a wealth of tips for introverts in his book, "*The Quiet Achiever: Tiny habits to have impact at work (without pretending to be an extrovert)*".[04] Tim's book is one of the best resources I've come across, and it's not just the practical tips that make it valuable. It's also presented in a very organized way, making it easy to digest.

Both of these resources provide excellent advice for introverts, empowering them to enhance their networking skills and feel more capable in social situations.

03. https://read.lowenergyleads.com/p/networking-for-introverts-conversations
04. https://www.thequietachievr.com

Networking will serve you for years to come

If you're like most people, you might have breathed a sigh of relief when you landed your job, thinking, "Finally! I'm done networking!" Most of us find networking to be a chore. But I hope I've helped show you that networking isn't just for job hunting and shouldn't be a chore. It's a valuable skill that will serve you for years to come.

Once you start seeing networking as part of your designer's toolkit, you'll stop thinking of it as a dreaded task and start seeing it as an opportunity to build better products. By keeping those meaningful connections close, you're not just keeping your options open but actively working to improve your team's operations.

You'll have a go-to group for quick advice, a heads-up about changes coming down the pipe, you'll learn about new opportunities, and maybe even a friendly ear when needed.

That's the power of a robust internal network!

Chapter 05

Survive and Thrive in a VUCA World

Have you found that things on your team are constantly in flux? Are stakeholders or product managers continually changing their minds? Does leadership change priorities daily?

Maybe you aren't getting access to users and are unsure what the right feature to tackle next is.Maybe there is so much to take in that you're having difficulty digesting it all.

You may understand one part of the larger system well but need help understanding certain aspects of the bigger picture.

You're not alone. In fact, it's common enough that there's an acronym to describe it all.

If you've experienced any or all of these problems, you live in a VUCA world.

W orking for a giant corporation has drawbacks, but there are also many great perks, including leadership training.

Years ago, I was nominated to attend a leadership training session at a fancy off-site in the Hudson Valley of New York.

I thought, "I'm a UX designer. What am I going to learn from these MBA people in suits? This is such a waste of my time!"

Boy, was I wrong?

The facilitators divided us into groups, and we played a game centered on space colonies that had to build and market spaceships. This unexpected experience turned out to be a transformative learning opportunity, opening my eyes to new perspectives and strategies.

They separated us into teams. Each team (company) was comprised of your standard business-type roles: The CEO, the CFO, the CMO, the CTO, and all the Chief [insert letter here] Officers. Each person on the team was responsible for some aspect of the business.

We had to collaborate. We had to strategize. We had to plan.

Throughout the game, the facilitators threw various scenarios our way that completely upended our plans.

We were forced to adapt fast. Sometimes, we had an hour, sometimes 30 minutes. Sometimes, they made us decide without consulting the rest of our team.

Ultimately, we failed miserably.

I learned about volatility, uncertainty, complexity, and ambiguity.

I changed that week. But I emerged from the game with a newfound understanding of my role as a UX designer and a deep appreciation for what our job truly entails.

What does all of this have to do with UX?

As we've stated so often in this book, "user Experience" is simply the experience a user has. And as you're no doubt aware by now, many things can impact that experience.

Remember, the entire team impacts a user's experience. The sales team sets the price. The engineering team can introduce bugs. The marketing team shapes the brand promise. Stakeholders determine the release schedules, and the product team sets the feature sets.

The larger team or organization can often control these things, even if the UX team doesn't control them directly.

However, the user's experience is shaped by factors entirely outside of the team's control: the user's environment, the user's internet speed, their hardware, and even their state of mind. There are other completely unknown factors we can't even imagine here.

Every day, we face changing variables, a lack of information, multi-faceted problems, and conflicting information.

We are living in a VUCA world, whether we realize it or not.

Suppose we don't learn to navigate all of this volatility, uncertainty, complexity, and ambiguity we face daily. In that case, it doesn't matter how well we name our Figma layers or how perfectly our typography is aligned to the grid.

What is VUCA?

The chances are good you've never heard the term "VUCA" before. If you have heard it, you've likely heard it in the context of corporate leadership training or books for executives. I doubt you've heard this in the context of software, let alone UX design.

Although the term 'VUCA' may be unfamiliar to many in the software and UX design fields, its relevance is undeniable. Understanding VUCA is crucial for navigating the constantly changing software and product development world.

VUCA stands for Volatility, Uncertainty, Complexity, and Ambiguity. It describes a constantly changing world that can be difficult to predict or understand. If that doesn't sum up the software and product lifecycle, then I don't know what does!

I worked at my last company for nearly eight years. Within that relatively short period, I had over 15 supervisors. The company had three different CEOs and went from a giant multi-national global conglomerate to selling each business into its separate entity. And still, my team had to continue to deliver great products. **That's volatility.**

Half the time I worked for my last company, we dealt with the fallout from the 737 Max debacle. Then COVID ultimately killed the travel industry. Customers stopped flying planes, which meant no one was paying for services. It was always one thing after another. **That's uncertainty.**

Massive orgs, massive systems, siloed teams, software that didn't connect, legacy software that had to connect to new tools the teams were building daily, large customers, small customers, commercial carriers, and shipping carriers. **That's complexity.**

Constant org changes and leadership turnover meant no consistent strategy, no metrics, and no way to tell if we were building the right thing. Big ideas were thrown around at the highest level, with no way of getting there. **That's ambiguity.**

Throughout all of this, we were expected to deliver.

You might think this is an isolated case because I worked for such a giant multinational corporate conglomerate. But things like this happen daily for UX Designers and software teams regardless of the size or scale.

This happens with small mom-and-pop design studios and at fast-paced startups. It doesn't matter if you're building B2B or B2C or any combination of these things.

It doesn't matter where you work.

I'm sure you've seen similar scenarios before. The challenges of VUCA are not unique to you or your team. They are simply a part of building software.

The great thing about VUCA is that some brilliant people have crafted frameworks that help us think more clearly about the problems and how to navigate them. These practical frameworks can empower you to tackle even the most challenging VUCA scenarios, which we will cover in this chapter.

You cannot always avoid these volatile, uncertain, complex, or ambiguous scenarios. But giving it a name and knowing what to look for can help you think more clearly about moving forward.

A Brief History of VUCA

It was first described in 1985 by two economists and university professors, Warren Bennis and Burt Nanus. In their book, "Leaders. The Strategies For Taking Charge," [01] they discussed the challenges posed to leaders by various external factors.

Planning for the eventual collapse of the USSR, the US Army War College started to use VUCA to navigate the changes that might result from new states popping up throughout the former USSR.

---

01. https://www.google.com/books/edition/Leaders/emy4zshg8jcC

The challenge for the US and its allies was to find new ways of responding in a multipolar world where new allies and enemies might appear from every corner without much warning.

These new countries had different political alliances. Some had leftover Soviet military equipment, and some had Soviet nukes! How might these new states react to the US and NATO? Would they align with the "West" and NATO, or would they align closer with less friendly countries like China and Iran?

That sounds pretty VUCA to me!

VUCA isn't one thing but four distinct things

It's common to conflate the four separate concepts into one. It's important to remember that VUCA is not one monolithic thing. It's more of a framework to understand how you might react to and mitigate issues based on the amount of information you have and how well you can predict something will happen.

Each of these four scenarios we will discuss can happen on their own. You may have a lot of one and a little of another. You may have a little of all. You may have a lot of all of them. You may only have one of them.

There is no monolithic VUCA scenario.

At the end of this chapter, you won't be able to prepare for VUCA. You will be able to prepare and be ready for volatile and uncertain, complex, and ambiguous situations separately. Each is different. And each requires different approaches to prepare and navigate them successfully. Ironically, VUCA itself is VUCA!

VUCA is not one thing. V, U, C, & A are all different scenarios.

Charting the VUCA scenarios

In 2014, Nate Bennett and G. James Lemoine published an article on navigating these various VUCA scenarios.[02] They created a framework from that paper to help identify and understand the best strategies and tactics for making better decisions when faced with these scenarios.

They created a simple four-blocker to explain these concepts.

On the Y axis is how well we can predict the results of an action we take. On the X axis is how much we know about the situation.

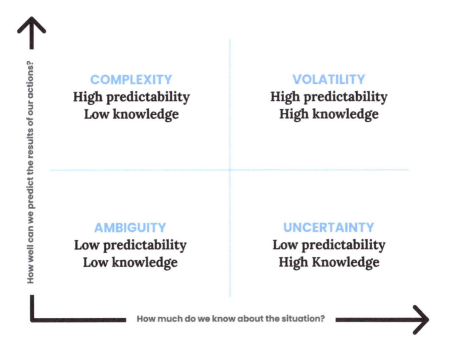

Using these four quadrants, we can successfully plan our different VUCA scenarios and navigate these unique challenges.

02. Bennett, Nathan and Lemoine, James, What VUCA Really Means for You (Jan/Feb 2014). Harvard Business Review, Vol. 92, No. 1/2, 2014, Available at SSRN: https://ssrn.com/abstract=2389563

Volatile

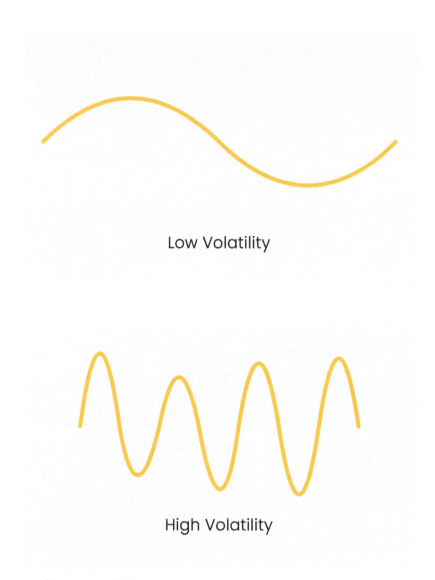

Copyright Jeroen Kraaijenbrink

For this and the following three sections I'm using illustrations adapted from Jeroen Kraaijenbrink for a 2018 Forbes article: https://www.forbes.com/sites/jeroenkraaijenbrink/2018/12/19/what-does-vuca-really-mean/?sh=2968ce1517d6

How do you manage a constantly changing environment?

Think about this common scenario you've likely dealt with before: a product team that can't seem to make up its mind. Every couple of weeks, a new feature is suggested. The team focuses on a new feature in one sprint but is asked to think about something new in the next sprint. In the next sprint, the product team has an entirely different idea.

You could just constantly pivot, changing direction every few weeks. But you know that is a mistake.

In a volatile environment, it's not that we don't understand one particular outcome over another. We have a pretty good sense of what is happening right now.

The problem is that things are just constantly changing.

Highly volatile environments are usually characterized by high predictability and high understanding. The problem here isn't that we don't know something or can't predict the future. The problem is that there are so many scenarios that we just don't know which scenario will play out to our benefit.

Look for rapid changes. These could be outside changes, like sudden market shifts, or they could also come from inside, like a stakeholder constantly changing their mind. It's not just about the change itself but the speed and scale at which it happens.

It might be simple, and it might not be hard to predict the outcome of individual scenarios, but constant change can keep us from making the right decision.

When things are constantly changing, there will surely be things you can't control. You can't control your team and what they will do or say. You can't control organizational changes, product direction, market conditions, or technology. It's essential to focus on what you can control.

Most importantly, you can control your mindset. How you react to constant change is just as important as anything. If you know things will constantly change, embrace your ability to adapt.

You can also control expectations. You may not be able to control everything, but you can ensure your team understands volatility's impact on your work. Change will undoubtedly impact your work, but you can't wait until the last minute to say something is wrong.

Here's what you can do to thrive in volatility

Volatility presents unique challenges, but you can effectively navigate these rapidly changing conditions with the right approach. We'll discuss methods for understanding the situation thoroughly, documenting your processes, staying informed about changes, building a support network, and developing contingency plans. These strategies will help you adapt quickly and maintain sanity despite constant shifts in the environment.

Understand the situation

Network internally to get as much information as you possibly can. Attend cross-functional meetings, even if you're not required to. Reach out to colleagues on other teams who might have insights that can help you.

Work to understand the unknowns. Figure out the known unknowns–those things you know you don't know–and work to understand those things.

Then try to think through what some unknown unknowns could be–All the aspects you haven't even considered yet. This might involve brainstorming sessions with your team or mentors to identify potential blind spots. Remember, in large organizations, your project might be impacted by decisions or initiatives you're unaware of.

Document everything

Keep detailed records of decisions and changes. Use tools like design systems, wikis, or simple shared documents to track what changed and why. This helps you track revisions and makes adjusting based on new directions easier.

When stakeholders suddenly pivot, or new information comes to light, you'll have a clear record of your thought process and can quickly identify which elements need reconsidering. Plus, this documentation becomes an invaluable resource for onboarding new team members or briefing executives who might need to become more familiar with the project's history.

Stay informed

Keep in regular communication with your team and stakeholders. This doesn't mean bombarding people with constant updates but establishing reliable channels for information to flow to the right people.

Set up regular check-ins, subscribe to relevant internal newsletters, and don't be afraid to ask questions–even if you think they're dumb questions. Stay updated on any potential changes, no matter how small they might seem. Being among the first to know can give you more time to adapt.

Find support

Chances are good you're not alone in dealing with constant change. Build a network of colleagues who are also struggling

Focus on what you *can* control, not the things you *can't*.

with the same changes. This could be within your organization or even in your broader professional community.

Share strategies and experiences. This helps provide practical insights and emotional support. Consider starting or joining a regular meeting or Slack channel where you can discuss the challenges and solutions.

Remember, while your specific project at work might be confidential, the strategies for dealing with change are often universal and shareable.

Always have a backup plan

Understand the potential outcomes of the known scenarios. This is an excellent thought exercise for preparing for one of those scenarios. But don't stop at just one backup plan—consider multiple alternatives.

What if your primary stakeholder leaves the company? What if your budget gets cut in half? What if a competitor releases a similar product before you? Thinking through these scenarios in advance means you're not just preparing for specific events. You're also training yourself to be more adaptable and quick-thinking when unexpected changes finally occur—and they will!

Share what you learn

Don't keep all this valuable information to yourself. If your team deals with volatility, they'll benefit from knowing what you know.

Consider setting up knowledge-sharing sessions where team members can present insights they've gained. Create a shared resource where people can contribute learnings and best practices. The internal network you've built will help to inform who needs this information and what they might need to know.

Uncertain

Low Uncertainty

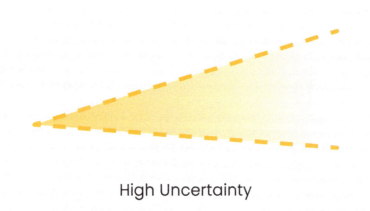

High Uncertainty

How do you manage an uncertain environment?

We've all encountered conflicting feedback, a company pivot, and a change in direction. It's a familiar scenario, but it can leave us questioning whether our work aligns with the bigger picture.

Think about this scenario you may have dealt with at a startup still finding its way: Two competing executives can't seem to agree about the company's mission. One influential executive thinks the company should go in one direction, while the other says it should go in another.

This decision puts the company at a crossroads and could change everything your team has been working on for the last year.

You aren't sure which direction is correct. You just wish leadership would decide so the team can get to work. The team is at a standstill. What's the next move?

In an uncertain environment, it's not that we don't understand what is going on. We may have a pretty good idea of the situation.

The challenge is in predicting what will play out over time.

Highly uncertain environments are usually characterized by low predictability but a high understanding of the situation.

In uncertain environments, the path forward isn't clear. We can understand many potential scenarios well, but we have no idea which one will play out. Or it's challenging to forecast future trends or outcomes because of a lack of reliable information.

There are many unknowns.

There are things we know, things we know we don't know, and things we don't know that we don't yet know.

These unknowns could be problems, opportunities, players, regulations, constraints, etc.

So, when there are many unknowns, start with what you do know. What is happening right now, and how is it impacting your team? Who do you know that might be able to help? Is there some way to move forward?

Work to understand what you know you don't know. Leverage your network. Knowing who to go to for an answer can save you lots of headaches—this is why internal networking is so important! Leverage your cross-functional team and break down any silos in your way.

As you work, constantly check yourself. Shop your ideas around and seek feedback. Focus on discovery to gain new insights. Experiment to uncover things you didn't expect. While you do this, keep an eye out for things you don't know you don't know.

Here's what you can do to thrive in uncertainty

While uncertainty can be daunting, there are practical ways to manage it effectively. We'll examine approaches to acknowledging limitations, maintaining flexibility, cultivating a growth mindset, setting clear expectations, and applying lessons from volatile situations. By implementing these strategies, you'll be better equipped to make decisions and progress in uncertain conditions, turning potential obstacles into opportunities for growth and new ideas.

You don't know everything

The unknown unknowns are everywhere. Don't get a big head and assume you have all the answers. It's okay not to know everything. Embracing your ignorance can be a powerful tool. Approach each problem with a sense of curiosity and humility. Ask questions, even if they sound naive.

By acknowledging what you don't know, you open yourself up to learning and adapting quickly. This mindset also makes you more approachable to colleagues who have valuable insights to share.

Be ready to pivot

Don't put all your eggs in one basket, making change impossible. Be flexible and willing to pivot when the time comes. Design your processes and solutions with flexibility in mind from the start. That could be using modular design principles or simply keeping your team agile and trained.

When building your timelines, include buffer time for unexpected changes. Most importantly, cultivate a mental attitude that doesn't see change as a setback but an opportunity to create something even better.

Have a growth mindset

You will likely be wrong at some point. It's not a matter of if but when. The key is how you respond in these moments. Learn what went wrong, work to fix it, and try to avoid similar mistakes in the future.

Treat each setback as a learning opportunity. Conduct post-mortems to gather insights. Share these learnings with your team and the broader organization. Learning and adapting quickly is often more valuable in uncertain environments than being right the first time.

Set clear expectations

The worst thing you can do is wait until the last minute to tell people that uncertainty impacts your work. Be as transparent as possible, as early as possible. If you see storm clouds on the horizon, don't wait for the rain to fall before you mention it.

Start with what you *do* know, and leverage your network.

Regular, honest communication about potential challenges or delays can help stakeholders adjust their plans and expectations. It also builds trust–people appreciate knowing where things stand, even if the news isn't ideal.

When communicating uncertainties, pair them with potential solutions or mitigation strategies to show you're proactively managing the situation.

Leverage strategies from volatile environments

Many things we discussed with volatile environments are essential here, too: Find support, keep your ear to the ground, and share what you know as soon as you learn it. Build a network of colleagues who can offer different perspectives and support. Stay informed about changes in your organization and industry that might impact your work. And when you learn something new, don't hoard that information–share it with your team and relevant stakeholders.

Information is a valuable currency in uncertain environments. By freely sharing what you know, you not only enhance your own value but also become an integral part of your organization's information network. This fosters a sense of connection and collaboration within your team and organization, making you feel empowered and essential.

Remember, thriving in uncertainty isn't about eliminating unpredictability. You'll never eliminate these things. It's about building your capacity to respond effectively to whatever comes your way.

Complex

Low Complexity

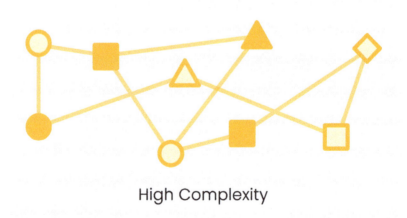

High Complexity

Is complexity something you only run into in enterprise orgs?

Complexity is an inescapable aspect of software development, whether in a startup or a large organization. Recognizing this inevitability is critical to preparing and building resilience.

When we think about complexity in software and design teams, we often think of a few things: Legacy systems built decades ago, large siloed orgs with conflicting priorities, cross-team dependencies across those large orgs, and much more. For instance, a complex problem in a software team could be managing a project with multiple interdependent modules, each with its own set of requirements and deadlines.

You'll run into complexity on smaller teams, too. At small startups, you might find heavy reliance on 3rd-party integrations. There might be tech and design debt from moving fast and breaking things. Smaller teams might be juggling multiple features for different personas all at once.

I worked for several years in a large global conglomerate. I had many different roles, but one stands out as one of the hardest I've ever had: working on a horizontal software team responsible for multiple business problems as a shared service.

Think inspection and repair of machines for gas turbines, jet engines, train locomotives, wind turbines, and, in theory, anything else this industrial conglomerate wanted to build.

We dealt with several P&Ls and the baggage that came with it. There were more stakeholders than I could count. There were too many personas and jobs to be done. Legacy systems and integrations needed to connect—so many timelines, roadmaps, and expectations from leaders across the various organizations

In a complex environment, it's not that we don't understand individual parts. We may have a good sense of the pieces.

The problem is that it's hard to digest the entire system together.

A highly complex environment is generally characterized by high predictability and low understanding. So, you can quickly determine how individual scenarios might play out, but there may be so many moving parts that it's overwhelming.

There are many moving parts in a complex environment. While you may understand individual aspects well, combining them makes them hard to digest. Multiple factors could influence each other, and each outcome could be relatively simple. But when everything comes together, we end up with a tangled web of cause and effect.

Try to look at individual problems on their own until you understand them. Then move on to the next. Then, understand how those things connect. Keep adding until you get a good sense of the big picture. Zoom out and in as necessary to keep the proper context.

Here's what you can do to thrive in complexity

We'll explore strategies to help you embrace this complexity rather than shy away from it. Remember that complexity isn't something you can avoid. Complexity is inherent in software, and you will be running into it constantly.

Embrace complexity

Complexity is unavoidable, especially in large organizations or intricate projects. Avoid overcomplicating things, but remember that making things too simple is a potential pitfall to avoid. Striking the right balance is vital.

When faced with a complex problem, resist the urge to simplify it immediately. Instead, take time to understand the nuances and interconnections. Sometimes, what seems like unnecessary complexity is a crucial part of the system.

By embracing complexity, you might discover new solutions that wouldn't be apparent with an oversimplified view. Your users and stakeholders may live in a complex world, and your solutions must reflect that reality.

Break the problem down

First, examine the individual problems and understand the pieces that make up the puzzle. Once you understand what's happening, work to understand how it's all connected.

This scenario is somewhat like putting together a jigsaw puzzle–you need to examine each piece first to understand how they fit together to form the bigger picture.

Start by listing out all the components of your problem. Then, dive deeper into each one. As you understand the individual elements, start mapping out how they interact. Look for cause-and-effect relationships, dependencies, and potential conflicts.

This approach makes complex problems more manageable and often brings new insights to the surface that might not be apparent when looking at the larger, more complicated whole.

Look for people who know the other parts

The chances are good that other people understand the individual pieces well, even if they don't understand the whole. Work with them to help you get up to speed. This is where your networking skills come into play.

Identify experts in related areas. Don't be afraid to schedule coffee chats or quick video calls to pick their brains. Most people are happy to share their expertise if asked.

When faced with a complex problem, resist the urge to simplify it right away.

As you gather insights from these different experts, you'll start to see connections they might see. You will become the connector who can see the big picture formed by all these individual pieces of the puzzle to carry along our puzzle metaphor.

Document Document Document

Information is our cheat code. Capture everything you know and make sure you're sharing this with everyone else. Don't create reports that no one will read, but think about how to document and share information in a valuable way. Maybe it's making a wiki, maintaining a shared Notion database, or even starting an internal podcast where you interview different experts.

The key is to make the information accessible and digestible. Use visuals like mind maps or flowcharts to illustrate complex relationships. Regular show-and-tell sessions can be a great way to share your growing understanding with your team.

Whatever you do, make sure you're documenting where your team already is. Don't expect your team to embrace a new tool, instead, decrease the friction as much as possible.

Don't be afraid to ask for help

Complexity can be overwhelming. If you're getting stuck, remember that seeking insights from others is not a sign of weakness. There's no shame in admitting you don't understand something. Reach out to colleagues, mentors, or even online communities. Frame your questions clearly, showing what you've already tried or what you know so far.

By reaching out, you're likely to build stronger professional relationships and uncover even more opportunities for collaboration with other teams. You'll also gain new perspectives and insights, which can be invaluable in a complex environment.

Ambiguous

Low Ambiguity

High Ambiguity

"Where do we start?!" Stop me if you've heard this one before.

Over eight years, I had fifteen different supervisors, my company went through three CEOs, I joined multiple businesses, and I dealt with countless leadership changes.

There was always volatility. There was always uncertainty. There was most definitely complexity. But the hardest one for me to get used to was ambiguity.

With volatility, you can account for the changes. With uncertainty, you can talk to more people. With complexity, you can dig in and figure it out.

But ambiguity? No one is there to give you the answers. Unfortunately, for the most part, you and your team are on your own to figure it out.

If complexity is the hallmark of large matrixed orgs, then ambiguity might be the hallmark of startups. You'll often hear things like: "We just need to ship something," or "We can refine it later," and without a doubt, "We'll just figure it out as we go!"

When it comes to ambiguity, our problem is that we lack a clear understanding and predictability.

Highly ambiguous environments are characterized by low predictability and low understanding. Our problem here is that we have incomplete or unclear information.

In an ambiguous environment, there are many unknowns. Relationships may be unclear. There may not be any historical precedents to reference. There are many unknown unknowns.

On software teams, we'll find that everyone has the same information. However, everyone seems to interpret this information differently.

Everything is fuzzy, and it's almost impossible to know what to do or which direction to take.

You'll likely never have someone telling you exactly what you should do. You'll likely never escape the need to figure it out as you go. You'll likely only have some of the answers before starting. Your best bet is to begin. If you don't know where to start, make your best guess and just start somewhere.

Do as much discovery as you can. Then, make your best guess. But just get started.

Work to get as much feedback as possible, as early and as often as possible. Then, correct the course and ensure you're not working too long without checking your work.

Talk to the right people to ensure you're heading in the right direction—whether that's a stakeholder, a user, or a colleague.

The worst thing you can do is head down a path for too long only to realize it was wrong.

Here's what you can do to thrive in ambiguity

Ambiguity is often characterized by unclear relationships, lack of precedents, and differing interpretations of the same information. This section will provide you with practical approaches to move forward despite incomplete information. We'll discuss the importance of taking action even when you're not 100% sure, seeking early and frequent feedback, and maintaining flexibility in your solutions. By implementing these strategies, you'll be better prepared to make decisions and progress in ambiguous environments.

You'll never be 100% sure

Embrace the idea that you'll never have all the answers. It's a liberating realization, really. Your colleagues will often feel as lost as you feel, so bring your unique ideas to the table.

Instead of striving for a perfect understanding 100% of the time, focus on making the best decisions with the information you have. In many cases, a good decision now is better than a perfect decision later.

Don't put off starting

Use the information you do have to make a best guess. It may not be the best answer, but now you have a data point of what doesn't work. The sooner you start, the sooner you'll know what's working and what's not.

Embrace action over endless planning. You might make mistakes, but those mistakes are valuable learning opportunities. Think of it as an experiment for your ideas. Each trial brings you closer to a solution that does work. By starting early, you give yourself more time to pivot if needed.

Don't delay feedback

Get feedback early and often. Treat your work like little experiments. Run assumptions past people who may have insights you don't. Ask them where you might be wrong. It's often easier to get answers once you put your ideas down on paper.

This approach serves multiple purposes. It helps validate (or invalidate) your ideas quickly and engages stakeholders in the process. This quick feedback often uncovers perspectives you hadn't considered.

Embrace the idea that you'll never have all the answers.

Don't wait until you have a polished product to seek input. Rough sketches, quick prototypes, or even articulated emails or messages are enough to start a productive dialogue.

Be flexible

Fall in love with the problem, not the solution. Don't tie yourself to any specific solution. Chances are good you'll need to pivot and change things up at some point anyway.

Always be open to new ideas and ways to solve the problem, even if they're not your ideas. This mindset allows you to adapt quickly when circumstances change or new information comes to light. Embrace ego-free problem-solving.

Your initial idea might be a stepping stone to an even better solution that emerges through collaboration. Embrace the ability to admit when you're wrong or someone else has a better idea.

Information is our cheat code

If ambiguity is a lack of information, then the more information you can get—whether through conversations, discovery, or experiments—is our goal. The more information you have, the more informed your next decision will be.

Your goal isn't passive information consumption. It's about active, strategic information gathering. Seek out diverse sources, ask probing questions, and always connect the dots. Information isn't just facts and figures. It's also understanding context, motivations, and potential future scenarios.

You're not just reducing ambiguity when you continuously expand your knowledge base. You're positioning yourself to better spot opportunities and avoid pitfalls that others on our team might have missed.

LET'S HEAR FROM THE EXPERTS

Tonja Barlow
Principal Voice User Interface Designer

Tonja shares her journey transitioning into AI conversation design, offering valuable insights on navigating VUCA.

With over 15 years of UX design experience, I dove into AI conversation design! This opportunity to create user experiences through content and conversation was my sought-after challenge. However, being new to conversation design...at a new company... in a new industry... and working with new teammates on a new virtual assistant made this venture a **volatile** move.

Onboarding onto a newly created team, some steps are necessary for problem-solving in a volatile environment:

Identify the Problem In a volatile atmosphere, requirements may be half-baked. Ask questions to clarify partners & scope.

What's the Project Goal Align the project with your organization's overall goals to establish a common directive. A shared goal enables better collaboration.

Find Alternative Solutions Consider risks, pros/cons & feasibility of each potential solution.

Determine the Best Solution Quick user feedback can inform design decisions. Justify your choices to solidify decisions in an ever-changing environment.

Execute on Solution & Monitor Implement quickly and track performance to determine effectiveness.

Review & Refine Assess effectiveness, review regularly, and refine to improve both solution and process.

With volatile circumstances came **uncertainty** in our virtual assistant's platform technology. Would it support the product vision? How would potential changes affect the current and future vision?

All of these uncertain questions needed to be addressed concurrently with the launch of our MVP. Even with roadmap uncertainty, there should be plans in place to help prioritize and mitigate risks involved with release plans and the potential change in platform technology.

Creating an impactful virtual assistant is daunting. NLP (Natural Language Processing), can be **complex** when launching a sophisticated assistant. Conversation design involves many intricacies: Natural Language Understanding (NLU), Natural Language Generation (NLG), slot types, entities, sentiment analysis, etc. Information organization was key in learning and teaching teammates the basics.

Conversation design is about **ambiguous** scenarios. For our MVP, we targeted low-hanging fruit, releasing simple intents for quick insight into improving engagement later.

Having no precedent created an ambiguous setting that enabled creative thriving. Questions like "Can voice input enhance the client's chat experience?" help establish design direction. The right leadership providing clear vision was crucial for our successful MVP launch.

Being able to actively listen to stakeholder requests as an empathetic designer; understanding the leadership vision; openness to learn and understand complex new logic; and being able to execute solid designs in an uncertain atmosphere are all skills that designers can benefit from in developing both better client experiences and establishing yourself as a design leader.

Courageous followership is critical for success

In these VUCA environments, your leadership team may be just as lost as you are. They may not have the answers. If you wait around to be told what to do, you may be waiting for quite some time. That's why courageous followership is so essential.

Individual contributors can't effectively navigate a VUCA environment without practicing courageous followership. In Chapter 8, we'll dive deeper into what being a courageous follower means for individual contributors, But for now, understand that at its core, followership is about being actively engaged, thinking critically, and caring enough about the mission and the team to voice concerns and offer constructive feedback when things aren't heading in the right direction.

Often, the qualities of courageous followership might be mistaken for leadership behaviors. This mix-up occurs because both share common traits such as initiative, decision-making, and accountability.

Much of this volatility, uncertainty, complexity, and ambiguity we discussed in this chapter is nearly impossible to navigate if you do not own your actions.

Many people on our teams will sit in the back seat and wait for someone above them to tell them what to do instead of taking charge and deciding on their own. These people will struggle when they encounter the issues discussed in this chapter.

Once you've read through Chapter 8, you'll better understand how embracing this concept will help you survive and thrive in a VUCA environment.

VUCA is not just for leadership training

Remember that this information is not just for CEOs or corporate leadership training. These concepts can be applied broadly to everyone on the software team, especially the design team.

I've found that the design team is often left out of important meetings, or things are handed down from various stakeholders without much warning. The result frequently combines many things we've discussed here for design teams. It doesn't matter where you work. I'm confident these scenarios are something you will run into at work.

The next time you're handed a set of requirements and something seems off, think about the four scenarios discussed in this chapter. Having the names and the framework we've discussed today will be an excellent place to start as you navigate VUCA throughout any career stage.

Good luck out there!

Chapter 06

The Art of Stakeholder Management

You've spent weeks perfecting your prototypes, aligning every element, and polishing every detail.

Then, out of the blue, a stakeholder throws a curveball–new requirements and different priorities—a complete pivot.

Suddenly, you're back to square one.

Sound familiar?

It's no secret that the term "stakeholders" often evokes a sense of dread in most UX designers.

But what if I told you "stakeholders" doesn't have to be a dirty word anymore?

What if I told you there's a way to navigate these changes and influence these stakeholders, too?

W hen I first started, I had a very antagonistic approach toward stakeholders. I often said things like, "Who is this person critique me? Don't they realize I am the designer?"

Stakeholders and designers often have a fraught relationship. It's no surprise that "stakeholder" has turned into such a dirty word. I often hear derogatory and negative conversations about stakeholders, which isn't helpful.

My perspective on stakeholders has evolved significantly since my early days. I now understand our vital symbiotic relationship. After all, if they fail, aren't we also failing?

I've lost count of how many stakeholders I've worked with throughout my career. Some were great. Some not so much. But two things are certain: Every stakeholder is unique, but each brings valuable insights we can't ignore.

Recognizing stakeholders as vital members of my team has been a game changer. Whether redesigning a current feature or launching a completely new product from scratch, understanding and effectively managing stakeholders will, without a doubt, make or break your project.

But who are these stakeholders? Why are they so important? And how can you, as an individual contributor, navigate the complex, often political nature of stakeholder relationships?

Taming the software team's often fraught relationships with stakeholders is not only possible. It's pretty straightforward, using some standard tools and frameworks that product managers and other teams have used for a while.

When you're done with this chapter, you'll be able to identify your stakeholder's needs, explore ways to communicate effectively, set the right expectations, manage their feedback, and, most importantly, build meaningful relationships.

So, what exactly is stakeholder management?

Stakeholder management may sound like something that your leadership team should be doing. And to tell you the truth, generally, this is something other teams are most likely doing. They're just not doing it within the context we'll discuss here.

The concept is crucial for UX professionals to understand because a mismanaged stakeholder relationship can kill even the best, most thoughtful ideas.

Stakeholder management sounds complex on the surface, and it can often be challenging, but at its core, it's relatively straightforward. It's simply a framework to better understand who is essential to your product and what they care about most.

Effective stakeholder management goes beyond simply identifying influential individuals. It requires building empathy for these stakeholders and meeting them where they are.

Stakeholder management involves identifying influential individuals and understanding and empathizing with their needs and expectations. It's about understanding their motivations and constraints, helping them achieve their goals, and influencing them to help you and your team achieve yours.

Who are our stakeholders?

The term "stakeholder" refers to the people who might be affected by the software. Or maybe they hold a stake—see what I did there—in the problem we're trying to solve. They may be the person who controls the budget. Generally, a stakeholder's opinion can impact the direction a team takes.

In its broadest sense, stakeholders can include anyone from product managers to executives, including marketing team members. They could also be customer service teams and sometimes even enterprise users–those people who have been tasked with helping to guide the development of the software from the business side.

Each stakeholder brings a unique perspective. They all have valuable insights and critical considerations regarding the product. Embracing this diversity of perspectives can lead to more effective discussions and a better product overall.

Stakeholders and how they interact with your team can vary wildly depending on your team and how your team works. But generally, they are individuals or groups with vested interests in the outcome of an individual feature or the software as a whole.

The team can decide who a stakeholder is. Still, this group can include team members like developers, product managers, fellow designers, clients, executives, and even end-users. Each stakeholder will have unique expectations, goals, and influence.

Stakeholders can often be an opaque group for ICs because, in many cases, product managers or other groups like supervisors or team leads will manage these relationships. So, as an IC this may not be a group you're familiar with.

The most important thing to remember is that stakeholders are not a monolith. They are simply people like you and me. They each come with experiences, opinions, biases, unique perspectives, and sometimes baggage.

Because of this, building a solid foundational relationship with this group can help us understand them better. When we understand these people better, we'll know the most effective ways to communicate with them. We'll know exactly what we need to communicate, exactly how to communicate, and we'll know precisely when to communicate.

So, just like building empathy for users, building empathy for your stakeholders is just as critical for your product's success.

Understand your stakeholders

Several years back, my team ended up with a new stakeholder who was supposed to help us understand the business side of some of the problems we were trying to solve.

It didn't take long for this particular stakeholder to start micromanaging. He was keenly interested in coming to scrum ceremonies like story grooming and planning, which was somewhat abnormal for this role.

It got to the point where he was micromanaging the engineering team and checking their work frequently. It got so bad that our product manager had to have a heart-to-heart and get this behavior to stop.

After talking with him briefly, we discovered that a previous team had burned him. They promised the world but didn't deliver, and he was put in a pretty tough spot because of it. So, this was his way of covering himself and ensuring the team did what they were supposed to do.

If we had made an effort to get to know this stakeholder earlier, this would have come up, and we would have been able to address his concerns before it got to the point that it did.

When a project kicks off, it's good to have a formal process, like stakeholder interviews or workshops designed to get to know your stakeholders. However, your relationship with stakeholders should always continue after that initial engagement.

In *Chapter 3*, we laid out the foundations of great software–great relationships. Stakeholder relationships are no different from those with the rest of our team.

In that chapter, I suggested 1:1s were the secret sauce to getting to know your team personally. Some stakeholders may not have the time for it if they're busy executives, for example, but if you can, I'd suggest regular or semi-regular touchpoints with your stakeholders, too.

It's a good idea to treat these 1:1s as informal interviews. Come prepared, ask questions, listen, and take notes.

Work to understand their expectations for the product or feature. Try to get a sense of what kind of pressures they're under. See what you can do to help them because helping them is helping you and your team.

Even if you're planning the more formal options for understanding your stakeholders, like stakeholder interviews, I suggest you keep the regular, informal 1:1s on their calendars to help build those interpersonal relationships as you work together over time.

These relationships with stakeholders will be invaluable when it comes time to have hard conversations later. And believe me, there will be hard conversations later.

A Symbiotic Relationship with Stakeholders

I often see design teams and outside groups like stakeholders being lumped into groups: It's us vs them! However, this type of thinking leads to in-group/out-group bias and can lead to many bad decisions made by everyone involved.

Our stakeholders are not the enemy; they're not a group we should consider defeating. In reality, we're all on the same team. If they lose, we lose. When they win, we win.

On the surface, you and your stakeholders come from entirely different perspectives. And it makes sense. Stakeholders often have a business-first approach. They may be driven by meeting business targets and achieving some organizational objective the UX team might not be aware of.

The UX team often has other things we're worried about, and we seem to speak entirely different languages.

Different backgrounds and points of view often seem to conflict, but they're also the key to building a symbiotic relationship. You and your stakeholders share a common goal: to create a product that solves user problems, ultimately driving business outcomes.

The stakeholder's and the UX team's overall goals shouldn't be that far apart, should they? They shouldn't be. If these things conflict, then something else is likely wrong.

This shared goal forms the foundation of your relationship with stakeholders. Remember that we often need the support of these stakeholders to achieve *our* goals. The stakeholders need the software team to achieve *their* desired outcomes or goals. We should never be working against each other.

Why is stakeholder management critical?

In the last chapter, I briefly discussed a product I worked on that was meant to digitize the inspection of components like jet engines and gas turbines. I mentioned that it was one of the most challenging jobs I've ever had. And just like with most software projects, this one was hard because of the people more than anything else.

Without getting into too much detail, we had a fantastic team, and we built some amazing things, but the software was canceled to help cut costs during COVID-19.

At the time, it was a shock. Considering how much money the shops saved using the software we were building, we didn't expect it. Thinking back on it more, it shouldn't have been that big of a shock. Our problem was that we didn't have the right people in our corner.

We hadn't engaged the people that held the purse strings. We were so focused on the one set of stakeholders that we forgot about the people we *didn't* have on our side. Someone else was in their ear, and those conversations were being had without us.

We were missing critical champions and allies who would have been in those important meetings where the ultimate fate of our product was being decided. We were on our own.

Stakeholder management can make or break your project. When executed well, it can smooth over even the most challenging problems your team will face.

When we cultivate deep connections with our stakeholders and understand what they expect and how we can help them, we gain deeper insight into what directly affects our work.

We may be able to understand forces outside of our control sooner, so we have more time to plan and react. It may give us insights into positioning our team to get much-needed resources. It also helps us gain insights into other stakeholders, so we know how to influence them to get what we need.

We have relationships with many people at work. Some of these relationships are good, some are beneficial, and some may improve things for the larger team, well beyond the UX team. Other relationships just don't seem to be very positive. Some may be inconsequential, and others are downright toxic.

With many of these relationships, we likely haven't put much thought and effort into them. They just are what they are. But many of these relationships can be cultivated and improved. We just haven't made the effort yet.

Stakeholder management is strategic relationship building. It's being intentional about these critical relationships with influential individuals.

Stakeholder management is understanding the landscape and identifying the people who can help us achieve our larger goals or, in some cases, keep us from achieving those goals altogether. Then, it's about planning how we communicate with these people. Our end goal is to improve the position of the product or team by utilizing these relationships in the most beneficial and effective ways possible.

However, ignoring this vital activity can have disastrous consequences for your team, as in the example I just highlighted.

Ignoring the feedback of essential people in your organization or other team members, not communicating appropriately with stakeholders, and not including those influential people in your planning can hurt you and your team in the long run.

Neglecting stakeholder management comes with significant risks. Ignoring this critical activity risks misaligned expectations. Lack of stakeholder buy-in can also lead to resistance and conflicts, resulting in derailment at best and defunding altogether at worst.

The UX team's role

As a UX team, our job is to understand users, champion their needs, understand their behaviors, and make sure our teams' address their pain points. We do the research and channel that empathy and understanding into conversations with the team. We create some designs or wireframes that we expect will meet whatever outcome the business sets. We work with the right team members to build it, and the code is pushed to production.

Pretty simple, right?

On the surface, it isn't all *that* complex, but throw some stakeholders into the mix, and complexity suddenly rules the day.

This complexity is where our job as UX professionals becomes somewhat muddy.

It's up to the UX team to be advocates for the users. It's also up to the UX team to understand the business needs and constraints. And it's up to us to balance those things and work with everyone else to achieve the best possible outcome for everyone involved. *Oof.*

The trick here is to strike a balance. Listen to our stakeholders, yes, but filter that information according to what we know our users need and our business wants. It's about evaluating how these various inputs align with what we know to be true based on the evidence.

Does their input add value to the experience or subtract from it? Is it based on evidence, or are they merely sharing a subjective opinion? Critical thinking will be incredibly helpful in determining this distinction.

Finally, before discussing strategies, remember that navigating stakeholder influence isn't a one-person job. And it's most certainly not the sole job of the UX team, especially not any single UX designer.

Stakeholder engagement is a team effort. It involves fostering an environment where everyone on the team, from the engineers to the product managers and everyone in between, understands and appreciates the value of each person's professional expertise.

This shared understanding is precisely why we reviewed relationship building and internal networking before discussing stakeholder management. We need these foundational relationships in place to manage our stakeholders effectively.

Managing these relationships is a daunting task on your own. So, if your team doesn't actively plan and actively work to manage stakeholder relationships, my advice would be to work closely with your product team to come up with a strategy with them. Don't try to do this all alone if you have a team to support you.

Assessment tools and frameworks

Looking back on our canceled product, we hadn't taken the time to consider the players outside our core team making decisions about which products received budget and which didn't.

We didn't have the right relationships with the right people to know that other tools were in the works to replace ours. We made decisions in a bubble, and we lacked the important context because we didn't make an effort to look at the entire system of decision-makers and how it affected us in the long term.

The key to an effective stakeholder management strategy is understanding who your stakeholders are, how much they care about the product, and how much power they have to change it.

First, we'll identify our stakeholders. Then, we'll determine their interest and influence. We'll assign them to groups and create a plan to keep them engaged, informed, or both. The overall process is straightforward. [01]

Assessment tools

Before we discuss strategies for managing stakeholders, let's consider some tools that help map what's going on and clarify the direction to take to improve how we work with this group.

---

01. Follow along at home. Download these templates online at beyondUXdesign.com/downloads.

All stakeholders are unique. Remember, these are individuals, not a monolithic group. Some might be resistant, some might be neutral, and too many just won't understand the value of UX or the software team. How do we navigate all of this?

Two tools that I like are the Stakeholder Engagement Assessment Matrix and a Stakeholder communication plan.

When we use these tools, they can become our guiding compass.

The Stakeholder Engagement Assessment Matrix, sometimes called an Interest-Influence Matrix, can help us plot stakeholders based on their interest in the project and their influence over what's happening. As we'll see in a moment, all of the high-interest, high-influence stakeholders are the people you need to engage and keep happy, and the stakeholders with low interest and low influence, we may only want to keep them informed.

A communication plan will help you plan how to keep these stakeholders in the loop. It's a great way to get all this information in one place and plan more efficiently.

Understanding who our stakeholders are, how much power they have, what they care about, and how they impact our work can give us a clear picture of what we're getting into. It'll also give us a clear idea of the current state and, eventually, what we should do to improve the situation if necessary.

Identifying and Understanding Stakeholders

Again, the UX team is not responsible for doing this alone. We should work closely with our team and go through these activities together.

If you're not on excellent terms with your product team, I recommend that you fix that relationship before you start working on stakeholder engagement. You'll likely have a lot of difficulty improving stakeholder relationships without your product partner's help.

Remember, building great software is a team sport!

Assessment Matrix

On my previous team, we left many stakeholder relationships to chance. We accounted for the stakeholders who were directly responsible for feature development, but we didn't account for the stakeholders beyond our core team.

Your stakeholders may be obvious, but for some teams, such as the team I was on, your stakeholders may be less clear, but think beyond your core team. This assessment matrix is a great way to account for those additional people and see where they fall.

Whether it's obvious or not, stakeholders will care about different things, and they'll each have different roles and responsibilities that give them more control over decision-making than someone else. Like with any system, it's pretty straightforward when you think about one or two stakeholders, but keeping track of it all is challenging when you add more and more stakeholders to the mix.

Let's look at the stakeholder assessment matrix to understand this. It allows you and your team to put this otherwise nebulous information down on paper and visualize. It'll help you understand who cares about your work and has power over its future.

A stakeholder could be very interested and supportive of your team and project. They may also be resistant for one reason or another. They may have some ideas and want to push them through. They may have misconceptions about UX or how software is generally built.

A highly influential stakeholder could need help understanding the project or the importance of what you're doing.

This matrix lets us take all the various stakeholders and identify the various combinations, which ultimately helps us prioritize the people we need to focus on the most.

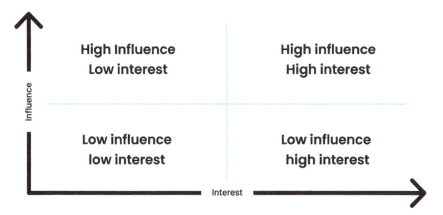

On the y-axis, we have their level of influence, and on the x-axis, we have their interest.

Once we understand a stakeholder's level of interest, we can assign them to four groups based on the quadrant they fall into. This grouping helps us to identify the best way to communicate and work with them.

Stakeholder Groups

Before we review the four stakeholder groups, it's worth highlighting that we're dealing with people. Each stakeholder is unique, so there are no monoliths here. This framework is meant to be a starting point to guide you in the right direction. However, remember that your stakeholders may have unique needs to consider.

By grouping stakeholders into these four buckets, we can quickly identify the what, when, and how to communicate with them.

The key to success is to know who cares about your work and who holds the power over its future.

Bystanders

If a stakeholder falls in the bottom left quadrant, they have low influence and low interest. These are our "bystanders."

These stakeholders are less involved and may have minimal impact on your team. You'll want to monitor them if their interest or influence changes, but they usually require less management.

We don't need to focus our attention on this group too much. We just want to keep an eye on them. *Our goal is to keep this group in the loop.* However, that doesn't mean we avoid them!

Supporters

If they fall in the top left quadrant, they are highly influential and low-interest. We'll call these "supporters."

This group has the power but might not be engaged with your work. It's crucial to keep these stakeholders satisfied and understand the value so they don't become obstacles.

Our goal is to try to satisfy this group. Engaging them enough to maintain their support without overwhelming them with details can be a balancing act.

Challengers

If they have high interest but low influence, they fall in the bottom right quadrant. These are "challengers."

These stakeholders are highly interested in your project but have limited power to change things. Despite this, they can be crucial sources of information and support.

Our goal is to maintain this relationship. It's a good idea to consult with them regularly to gain insights and build advocacy.

Champions

If they are in the top right quadrant, they have high interest and high influence. These are your "champions."

These stakeholders care deeply about what you're building and have the clout to influence it if they want to. Keep them in the loop with regular updates, and ensure you hear them out. Their input can be a goldmine, and keeping them happy can make your work much easier for your team. This regular communication shows that you value their input and respect their perspective.

It's crucial to keep your 'champions' closely engaged and informed. This involves addressing their needs and concerns, as they are key to the success of your project.

Here's what this matrix looks like visualized on paper.

SUPPORTERS

They may resist the project but can become supporters if engaged properly.

Our goal is to try to satisfy this group.

CHAMPIONS

They fully back the project and have the power to make things happen.

Our goal is to keep this group engaged.

BYSTANDER

Not deeply involved but need to be kept in the loop about the project's goals.

Our goal is to keep this group in the loop.

CHALLENGERS

Their support is key for a positive working environment.

Our goal is to maintain this relationship.

Influence

Interest

Filling out the matrix

Start by jotting down everyone involved or affected by your project. Think clients, team members, executives, users, etc. In our example, we'll use the CEO, the CTO, the head of marketing, a Product Manager, and the Lead Developer.

Place each stakeholder on the matrix based on their levels of influence and interest. For example, a stakeholder with high interest and high influence would go toward the top-right.

Remember, you should be working with your partners here, but it's not uncommon for the team to have disagreements and different perspectives about where individual stakeholders might fall. It doesn't matter if you can't come to a complete agreement.

What matters more is that you're having the conversation, and you're actively thinking about it. Remember, you can always revisit this matrix later if needed.

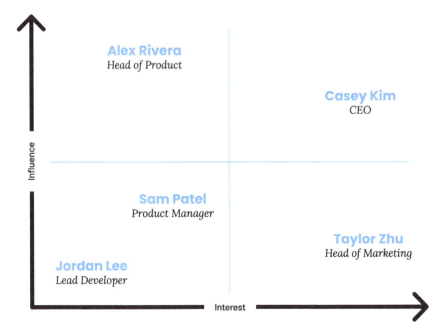

Understand that our stakeholders can be fluid. Depending on the situation, they can move between quadrants.

You may have a stakeholder who gets a promotion and gains more influence as they move up the ranks. As stakeholders move up the ranks, it's also possible that they become less involved and have less interest in this specific product.

It's also possible that different stakeholders can be in different quadrants depending on the various products. The head of marketing may have more influence over an external product than they might over a tool used only for internal purposes. So, depending on your scenario, you may have different maps for different projects. Just remember that these things are fluid and should be revisited semi-regularly, at the very least.

Once we understand our stakeholders and their interest and influence, we can think about how to communicate with them.

Remember, you should be working with your partners here, but it's not uncommon for the team to have disagreements and different perspectives about where individual stakeholders might fall. It doesn't matter if you can't come to a complete agreement.

What matters more is that you're having the conversation, and you're actively thinking about it. Remember, you can always revisit this matrix later if needed.

Communication Plan

When it comes to relationships, most people care about a few things more than anything else. They want to feel seen. They want to feel heard. They want to feel understood. These words of wisdom from a past guest on my show, Caden Damino,[02] hit home

---

02. https://www.beyonduxdesign.com/episode/85-goodbye-meetings-hello-design-time-with-ca-den-damiano/

that stakeholders are people, and our relationships with them aren't unlike any of our other relationships.

Each stakeholder will care about something different. They may prefer different communication channels, and they will most likely not attend every meeting you throw on their calendar.

We want to ensure each stakeholder feels seen, heard, and understood, but how do we do that?

With a thoughtful communication plan.

Creating a stakeholder communication plan is crucial in ensuring the success of any project. It involves a structured, thoughtful approach to thinking about how to communicate with your various stakeholders. We want to make sure the team aligns with their specific needs and interests, we communicate with them in a way they like to communicate, and we reach them when they need to be reached.

Many teams will default to either overcommunicating everything or communicating only when an issue arises. Either extreme is bad.

I can't stress enough that stakeholders are not a monolithic group. They all have different opinions, preferences, and ways they want to stay in the loop. This plan will help you and your team plan around those individual personalities and communicate as effectively as possible.

A communication plan can look as simple as this.

Name	Group	Key interests	What do we address?	Channel	Frequency

Filling this out is pretty straightforward.

→ In the first column, we have the stakeholders.

→ In the second column, we'll reference their group (challenger, champion, supporter, or bystander).

→ In the third column, we'll identify what we think they care about most. These could include organizational priorities, metrics, turnaround time, etc.

→ In the fourth column, we'll decide what to address with them. These are, of course, related to their interests, but we want to get more specific. If they care about ROI and business goals, we'll want to present a strong business case with a clear ROI when communicating with them.

→ In the fifth column, we'll list the channels we'll communicate.

→ Finally, we'll list how often we'll communicate.

When you're done, it may look something like this:

Name	Group	Key interests	What do we address?	Channel	Frequency
Casey	Champion	ROI, Business Goals	Strong business cases w/ clear ROI	Board Meetings	Quarterly
Alex	Challenger	Resource Allocation	Technical concerns in detail	Email	Bi-weekly
Taylor	Supporter	Timeline & Roadmap	Research findings & analytics data	Team Meetings	Monthly
Sam	Bystander	Research & Branding	General updates	Slack Updates	As Needed
Jordan	Bystander	Tech specs & timelines	Clear requirements & timelines	Daily stand-up	Weekly

Adapting Strategies

Sometimes, your stakeholders get shuffled around. They may leave the team, and someone else will be brought in to backfill their role. Sometimes, the thoughtful plan you created simply won't work, and you need to change strategies.

The information you use to complete these two tools is only a snapshot in time. Someone's influence may change. A stakeholder's interest can change. Their attitude can change. They may move to a new role, and they'll no longer be responsible for this product. Outside factors can also influence these things. It's impossible to say.

Remember to revisit and update these documents regularly. When something changes, you may need to adapt your strategy.

The two tools we reviewed here are just some of the tools at your disposal. A quick Google search will return an array of frameworks and templates. They're all about the same, and there isn't necessarily one that will always work better for every team every time. Experiment with the available tools and find a toolkit that works for you and your team.

All of this doesn't have to be complex. For some teams, the simple act of thinking about all of this is helpful. In reality, this is more than many teams ever do, so the fact that you and your team are putting any thought and effort into this idea puts you ahead of most teams.

Remember, we want to focus our efforts on the people with high influence and high interest. We especially want to convert the high-influence stakeholders with a negative attitude toward our work because these people can make life difficult for us.

LET'S HEAR FROM THE EXPERTS

Thomas Wilson
Director of Experience + Service Design + Strategy

Learn about how we might better understand stakeholders and power dynamics, especially on large and low-maturity teams.

In order to properly manage stakeholders, especially in an organization of lower or questionable strategy and design maturity, we need to do three types of artifacts.

01 Stakeholder list that is well categorized, using color for power or threatiness to the project.

02 Stakeholder map of all of those players and indicating their need to be core team, involved, informed

03 A power map of each internal system for every project and sometimes around each important stakeholder

04 SECRET Mapping: Create light personas associated with these maps to better understand people's social, religious, education backgrounds and define their motivations and beliefs. These are called 'secret' for a reason. Do not share these outside your immediate team or sometimes yourself. These are helpful in large orgs, large projects or heavy political environments. *Be careful about who has access.*

Remember, external maps of customers like Journeys and Blueprints are for understanding customer interaction and touchpoints within our system and service. These maps are for internal political power understanding and navigation.

It's also critical to understand networking.

→ *Informal network:* A map of the relationships that coworkers or others within a group form, like a clique and even, like a shadow org within an organization. Informal networks often, do not reflect formal hierarchies.

→ *Network centrality:* Describes how influential someone is in their network. Centrality can be measured in a few ways. One way is by identifying who is sought after for advice.

Power Mapping: The most important question to answer is: *Who controls access to what people value? And What do people value?* Who's under-appreciated or under-utilized but influential? Who brokers, controls or bridges information. Importantly who bridges disconnected groups. Who are the arbiters of culture and influence? What we have observed, in other words, is that learning who goes to whom for advice can tell us much more about who has power in an organization than the formal organizational chart by itself can. People to whom others go for advice are central in their organization's informal network. Do your coworkers see you as central? Do your projects and initiatives get endorsed by the people above you and are they received well by the people you work with or manage?

To build a power map—identify who has power in a setting and who doesn't—you need to answer two questions: What do people value? And who controls access to the valued resources? Answering these questions will help you identify the key players in a given organization, the resources they value, the resources they control access to, and the coalitions that exist among them.

Doing these things will ensure you have a great grasp on how information, power and influence moves throughout the organization. It will allow you to be the master electrician that harnesses that power in a meaningful way to get your needs met.

Strategies for good stakeholder relationships

Influencing our stakeholders' attitudes is a crucial part of this process. The result could be turning a resistant stakeholder into a supportive one or, better yet, a leading one.

Things like regular engagement, being completely transparent, clear communication, highlighting quick wins, and demonstrating the value of what we're doing can gradually influence their attitudes over time.

Strategy 1: Learn to speak the language of the business

I had a particularly difficult relationship with a stakeholder early in my career. In meetings, it was clear that they didn't care much for me or what I had to say. I would bring up something about the importance of users or design principles, and these things would get brushed aside. "We'll table that for later" is something he'd often say. Of course, we never revisited these things.

It wasn't until later that I realized my language was not resonating with this person. I used UX jargon and words this person likely had never heard before.

It wasn't that we had different concerns or priorities. We cared about the same things. My problem was that I wasn't translating in a way that made sense to him.

Not every stakeholder is going to be a "business" person. Some stakeholders will be software folks. Some could be customers. It's hard to say for sure. But if you're working in enterprise software or even some business-focused startups, someone may be on what we might call "the business side"–Someone assigned to a product or problem space as a subject matter expert.

If someone like this is assigned to your product, especially if they have never worked with software teams before, they might think they are the only ones who could possibly understand what the business needs or wants.

It may take some time to build trust, so learning to speak the language of your business will help add credibility. Understanding your business partner and using shared language will help build trust between your team and these stakeholders.

We often underestimate the power of shared language. This shared language can help combat the in-group/out-group bias frequently seen on teams. When you're conscious of how it works, it can be an effective way to break down barriers. Use it to your advantage, but don't be evil!

Work to understand how your business does business, how it makes money, who is in charge, and what they care about.

Understanding this can empower your team to navigate, communicate, and align work with those business goals. It'll go a long way in overcoming some of the challenges posed by stakeholders who may not fully understand software teams.

Needing to align your stakeholders is a perfect example of when we should use different storytelling techniques to show how what we're building ties to important business goals. Articulate the "why" behind your decisions over the technical specificities that may confuse them.

Kate Pincott gave a wonderful talk called *Name and Reframe* at designFAO about reframing the way we speak to get the rest of our team aligned with us. [03]

Speaking the language of the business can help us advocate for our work. We can tie those user problems to potential business impacts. Think about increased customer loyalty, market

03. https://www.youtube.com/watch?v=CLodJO4svc4

differentiation, retention, increased sales, or whatever the business cares about. We can make a compelling case for why our solutions are not just good for users but ultimately good for the business.

Strategy 2: Data as a Tool

Stakeholders are an interesting bunch. Big ideas and novel visionary concepts might influence some stakeholders. Some will expect you to show them the data and the objective proof.

Key metrics and data are prominent tools in our toolbox that can significantly influence stakeholder decisions. Data can help transform conversations from opinion-based to evidence-based and subjective to objective.

To do this effectively, we must make data collection and analysis an integral part of our design process. There is no avoiding it.

Gather as much information about your product and users as possible through observational discovery, such as ethnography, usability studies, surveys, interviews, quantitative analytics, and other key business metrics. Understand user behaviors, their pain points, and the impact this has on business outcomes.

Once we have all that data, keep it from sitting in a shared drive, gathering dust. Use it! Use this data to inform your designs, decisions, and discussions with the team when you present a design to stakeholders. Back up what you suggest with data. Explain why you've made certain design choices based on what the data tells you.

An easy way to do this is to highlight a statistic or a quote from recent research on a slide as you present. You don't even have to call it out explicitly. Although you certainly can if it makes sense.

This strategy requires you to be adept at gathering data, interpreting it, and presenting it. Remember to tell a compelling story about what the data says, then show how your designs fit into that important narrative.

Our stakeholders are most likely not designers and may be unfamiliar with UX techniques or terminologies. So, it's essential to present your data in a way that's easy to understand and clearly shows the link between the data, the design decision, and the business outcome. Don't talk about the how or the what on the screen. Talk about the why.

Remember, though, that every stakeholder is unique. Some might be wowed with sexy visuals, and others will want to see the numbers. It's essential to understand your stakeholders and what they care about.

Strategy 3: Setting Expectations

Relationships often go south for one straightforward reason. People make assumptions about the other party, and we don't live up to those assumptions. Animosity is usually the end result.

An easy way to avoid this is to set expectations early.

When I start working with a new stakeholder, there is something I do every time, without fail. I will set up a 1:1 and have an informal chat—I'm sure this isn't news to you. I've talked about the value of 1:1s throughout this book.

I will use the time to ask if they've ever worked with a UX team before and try to get a sense of how much they've been involved with software teams in the past, which is the normal stuff I've talked about already. This conversation helps me with context.

Here's the important part: I set expectations about my role, and this is something that I never skip.

Here's what I say:

→ Here's how I work.

→ Here's how I provide value to the team.

→ Here are the types of things I will deliver.

Once I've done that, I ask them what they expect from me or someone in my role. I want to get a sense of their perspective on those same three items.

After that, I ask them what their expectations are for their role. I will follow the same format I used: How do you like to work? Where do you think you'll add the most value? And What types of activities do you expect to be involved in? (Stakeholders don't usually have many deliverables).

I'll then work to establish what I expect from them. Instead of being direct, I will usually use examples from the past. So, for instance, I might say: "In the past, I've worked with stakeholders that did [insert the activity]. Does that sound like something you'd do too?"

This part of the conversation is a great way to remove ambiguity from the relationship. Going forward, you'll have a clear idea of what to expect from them and what they can expect from you.

I can't stress this enough: *You must manage expectations early!*

Expectations, unfortunately, are something many designers overlook. Setting expectations early will often keep you from having to do damage control later.

Setting expectations means being transparent about the roles and responsibilities of the software team and the stakeholders. Stakeholders need to understand the expertise that each party brings to the table. Your team should be upfront about what the stakeholders can expect from you.

Setting expectations becomes challenging when the product team isn't aligned here. So remember that having the product team on board with this strategy is essential.

But this goes both ways. Determining what you and your team expect from the stakeholders is just as important. Expectations could be set around what you need from them to be successful, how they will be involved, communication channels, delivery dates, what they can expect to see, who will approve changes, how late changes can be made, etc.

Strategy 4: Fostering Stakeholder Inclusion

I've seen too many design teams that treat stakeholders more like their "phone-a-friend" lifeline than actual members of the team. This usually looks like asking a question in a meeting, sending an email for feedback, and ultimately presenting a finished concept in a meeting.

More often than not, this is the first time stakeholders see it.

When you do that, you open yourself up to a ton of risk. There is a chance that stakeholders won't be on board with your ideas, but you won't know until the day of the big reveal.

A better idea is to bring your stakeholders along for the ride.

Some stakeholders will have zero interest in being involved, and others will want to be intimately involved. But be careful because stakeholders who expect to be involved may end up causing all kinds of trouble if they aren't included constructively. The key is to include stakeholders correctly and at the correct times.

Start by introducing them to the process.

Some stakeholders have an excellent working understanding of how software is built, while others may have never done this before and may need guidance if this is their first time working with a software team.

Stakeholder involvement could be as simple as explaining what the teams do, what the different roles are responsible for, why it's essential, and how it all contributes to the product's long-term success. It could also be more involved, like involving them in discovery and research trips.

Educate them about different methods and techniques—in a non-patronizing way, of course. Help them understand the value of these methods and how they inform your design decisions.

This method works best in 1:1s or small group settings. It's best not to "educate" a stakeholder in a large group setting, as they may resent being called out in front of peers and colleagues.

Once stakeholders understand the process better, invite them to participate when it makes sense. Invite them to participate in a discovery trip, and, when appropriate, include them in other activities. Let them see the challenges users face and how our decisions address them.

An important concept to consider here is the IKEA Effect.[04] This idea says that we tend to value something more if we have a hand in making it. The IKEA Effect is true for flat-packed furniture, and it's true for things like software, too.

Involvement can help them understand the "why" behind your design decisions and appreciate the rationale behind them better—without you having to explain anything.

Involving stakeholders in the process can also help mitigate the risk of disagreements or surprises later. When we include stakeholders in the process from the beginning, they're more

04. https://thedecisionlab.com/biases/ikea-effect

likely to be on board with the decisions made because they were a part of that process!

Stakeholders may be less likely to feel the need to push back because they've seen the evidence and the reasons behind each decision. If you do it right, they will feel like they helped make those decisions as part of the team.

Manage this inclusion carefully. It's not about giving stakeholders free rein over the process. It's about constructively involving them *at the right time* and *in the right way*.

Strategy 5: Make them feel seen, heard, and understood

I've already said it multiple times in this book, but I'll repeat it because I believe it's that important: **You cannot build great software without great relationships.**

If you take away one thing from this entire book, this is it.

Earlier in this chapter, I noted the importance of ensuring that your stakeholders—and everyone on your team—feel seen, heard, and understood.

At the heart of it all, stakeholder management is all about people. It's about understanding the people. It's about understanding their motivations and all their concerns. It's about understanding their communication styles so our team can effectively communicate with them. It's about ensuring your communication addresses their concerns and pain points.

As UX designers, we talk a lot about user empathy, but I can't tell you how seldom UX professionals display empathy for their team. Empathy is especially important for stakeholders.

Work to build empathy for your stakeholders. Understand the pressures they might be under, the targets they might need to meet, or whatever expectations they need to fulfill.

It will be tough for you to do this if every meeting you have with your stakeholders is full of 30 people multi-tasking while you present an 80-page slide deck.

If you want your stakeholders to feel seen, heard, and understood, try having smaller 1:1 meetings where you present ideas, get feedback, and discuss individually.

The chances are good. Having several thirty-minute 1:1s will be way more effective in selling your ideas, finding common ground, and generally moving the work forward than a single hour-long meeting with everyone on the team.

Stakeholders are not enemies to fight with

Some time ago, I interviewed the one and only Tom Greever. In that interview, we discussed the language we use and how so much of our language at work revolves around metaphors that relate to battles and fighting:

- ✕ Roll with the punches
- ✕ Fight for something
- ✕ On the front lines
- ✕ The hill to die on
- ✕ In the trenches
- ✕ Under the gun
- ✕ Battle plan
- ✕ Cutthroat

Another phrase we often use is "Divide and conquer," which strikes me as odd when discussing people you work with. This language is especially troublesome when discussing a group of stakeholders you need to manage.

I left this for last because this is such an important point. Stakeholders are not your enemy.

Building strong, positive relationships with your stakeholders can foster an environment of trust and mutual respect. When this happens, stakeholder influence is less likely to become an obstacle and more likely to become a valuable and, dare I say it, trusted resource.

It can also lead to constructive discussions, collaborative decisions, and, ultimately, a better user experience.

Remember, building great software isn't an isolated function. It's a team sport! It involves users, designers, engineers, product teams, and, yes, stakeholders too.

And when we manage it well, stakeholders can be powerful allies in our quest to deliver truly great software.

Follow along at home

Get the assessment matrix and communication plan templates online at *beyondUXdesign.com/downloads*.

Chapter 07

Dealing with The Challenges of Low Design Maturity

Imagine a software team where priorities seem to shift unpredictably, decision-making is ad-hoc, and stakeholders overstep their roles, micromanaging areas beyond their expertise.

Where roles aren't clearly defined, and there's no clear communication.

Imagine a team where engineers build what they want, where there's no collaboration, and technical limitations will override UX decisions.

You've likely experienced some or all of these things, and while they are often the norm, they shouldn't be. These aren't just "the life of a UX designer; " they are symptoms of low design maturity.

Is there anything you can do about it?

T ake a second to picture a product team that is consistently missing deadlines. Budgets and timelines are usually way off. Generally, nothing gets done on time, and things always cost more than anyone thought they would.

There are no objectives or goals. The roadmap is simply a list of disconnected features. Or worse, there is no roadmap at all. There's no strategic vision. There aren't any metrics for success. There is a lack of clarity around roles and responsibilities, leading to overlapping work or critical tasks falling through the cracks.

There is often an overemphasis on speed, delivering features quickly at the expense of quality.

Priorities change seemingly out of nowhere, with no apparent communication as to why. Constant change and lack of communication confuse everyone on the team. It will most likely lead to delays and rework. Decision-making is ad hoc, causing frustration for everyone involved. As decisions are reversed or changed, the design and engineering teams rework.

No one is given time to plan for the future. Everything is done quickly with little insight from people in critical roles like engineering or UX leads.

Product managers have a hard time saying "no" to stakeholders. They'll give in to whatever someone "important" says. Dates, resources, and features are up for grabs.

Stakeholders constantly interfere. They might push the team to avoid best practices and lean on immediate fixes rather than longer-term, more sustainable solutions. They might try to position themselves as subject matter expert or executive and push for unrealistic deadlines. Stakeholders may try to overstep their roles. They may dictate terms to the software team or micromanage aspects outside their domain expertise.

Stakeholders might push for their agenda without considering the potential impact on the user experience, the overall project outcome, or business outcomes.

There is little cross-functional collaboration. You'll probably hear, "We're not ready for UX yet" or "We're not ready for wireframes yet. We're still trying to figure out what we need." You won't get added to essential meetings, and your team won't communicate.

You won't be doing much discovery if you're allowed to do any in the first place. Instead, you'll get a list of specific requirements and, worst of all, most likely, a quick turnaround time. If discovery is done, it won't be done with any sense of rigor. The product managers or stakeholders will likely do it alone. UX-related work is inconsistent. If it is done, it's done haphazardly, and there are no repeatable standards.

There may not be an official UX function at all. If you're a UX designer, you may report to an engineering leader or a product manager. If your organization has an official UX function, it might have one or two champions. But it's not widely supported.

Since roles overlap, you might struggle with unclear expectations because of poor role definition within the team.

You may frequently have to revise your work because of shifting priorities. It may be hard to know when you need your work done, let alone what type of work will need to be completed. Different engineers may have different expectations when it comes to what they need to do their job. They may expect it at different times. They may or may not want you in their meetings.

Often, technical limitations will override UX. Engineers will prioritize what's easy for them. They'll make design decisions based on what's easiest to implement rather than what's best for the users, and they likely won't communicate those decisions to anyone, especially you, the UX Designer.

Engineers will ignore wireframes or prototypes completely. They may build whatever they want. Or if they do reference the designs, they might ignore parts of them.

On the other end of this problem, you might see a strict emphasis on a handoff, where designers have to spend time speccing every component and UI element instead of a standard design system or more collaboration, so you and your team will spend more time doing non-value-added work.

It's hard to know who to talk to when you see a quality issue.

Once a feature is pushed to production, no one will think about it again. They won't bother to get feedback, but not having OKRs or goals means there won't be anything to judge what would have made a successful release anyway. So... win?

There might be a few superheroes that everyone depends on to save the day, but without them, everything falls apart.

Your team is a feature factory. They're constantly working to release anything and everything hoping *something* sells.

People are overworked, and no one seems to be allocated to the correct projects. Everyone is OK with the status quo, and maybe worst of all, no one on the team is interested in improving.

Unfortunately, these challenges are not unique to your team. They are prevalent in most software teams. It's crucial to understand that these issues, while not acceptable, are often the norm. They are not just the way things are. They are symptoms of low maturity. Chances are, you're not alone in experiencing some or most of these challenges in your workplace.

These challenges are not theoretical. They are real issues, and are directly addressed in Nielson Norman Group's UX Maturity Model, particularly stages 2, 3, and 4. This model is a practical tool that we'll dig into shortly, providing you with a structured approach to understanding and addressing these issues.

Many people lament low maturity, and rightly so, but there's some good news in all of this. Low maturity isn't a death sentence for your career. You still have ample opportunity to deliver great work in this environment. You'll just have to do a little more work than you thought.

Low design maturity is not an IC's responsibility

Low design maturity doesn't happen in a vacuum. It's nearly impossible for a team to have high design maturity when the product or engineering teams have their problems unrelated to design. So, design maturity is just one aspect of a team's overall operational maturity.

The problem with this conversation around maturity is that it's generally seen through a leadership lens. Most solutions to low maturity are related to overall operations and how the teams function together–processes, resources, budgets, timelines, etc.

Maturity is, *without question*, a leadership problem.

However, the fact that this is a leadership problem is of little consequence to individual contributors who see this leadership issue manifest itself as just another crappy job.

ICs are left to deal with these symptoms on their own, with little support from leadership. Every. Single. Day.

The trouble is that they often don't realize it's a symptom of low design maturity. Too many, especially new designers, simply assume this is the chaotic life of a UX designer.

But fear not! I'm here to relieve you of that internalized stress and burden. You should not normalize this chaos. Low design maturity isn't a death sentence, and there IS a better way to work. I wrote this chapter to help you get there.

Since design maturity can be such an abstract term, instead of discussing design maturity in the abstract, I want to frame low maturity around the symptoms of low maturity you see daily.

We'll pick a few of these scenarios. Then, we'll discuss how you can work with your core team to deliver great work, even if the larger team is still a total mess.

Understanding design maturity

As UX professionals, you'll hear a lot about design maturity because you're on the UX team, but there are many other maturity models, too. Design maturity is just one small part of the larger software team's overall maturity. There are maturity models and corresponding levels for all kinds of things related to the software team. There's the Capability Maturity Model and the product management maturity model. There are maturity models for agile, data, DevOps, and many other processes.

In this chapter, we'll discuss low design maturity through the lens of Neilson Norman Group's maturity model. Still, when it comes to design maturity specifically, there are many different maturity models here, too. The Nielson Norman Group model is the most popular, but Jared Spool has a maturity model. UX Matters has a maturity model. InVision had a maturity model.

Each of these maturity models has different levels and criteria around what they define as a low design-maturity organization.

For this chapter, I will reference the Nielson Norman Group model, not because I think it's remarkably better, but because it's probably the most popular, so it's likely the one you'll find most people talking about when they reference "design maturity." So, for simplicity, I'm referencing this one, but remember, this is just one of several floating around.

How do we define design maturity?

Design maturity, at its most basic level, describes how much or little teams understand, value, and implement UX-related work or concepts. As the team understands, defines, builds, and releases software, it's how integrated activities we would think of as UX activities are into the overall process.

Let's look at the Nielson Norman Group model Jakob Nielsen developed in 2006.

Nielsen's scale has six stages:

01 **Absent:** UX is ignored or nonexistent.

02 **Limited:** UX work is rare, haphazard, or lacking importance.

03 **Emergent:** The UX work is functional and promising but done inconsistently and inefficiently.

04 **Structured:** The organization has a semi-systematic UX-related methodology that is widespread but with varying effectiveness and efficiency.

05 **Integrated:** UX work is comprehensive, effective, and pervasive.

06 **User-driven:** Dedication to UX at all levels leads to deep insights and exceptional user-centered–design outcomes.

NN/g's Survey Results

I like referencing this particular model because Nielson Norman Group does an ongoing survey to see where various UX and design organizations fall.

Unfortunately, as of this writing, they haven't released new results since January 2022. However, changing a team's culture and improving maturity can take years. The chances are good these results would be relatively the same today, although many new design orgs have been spun up since January 2022. This fact is just something to keep in mind. But of course, the fact that these results are old is something to keep in mind.

Let's analyze the most recent results: [01]

→ **Stage 1**, absent, was only about 1%.

→ **Stage 2**, limited was about 17%. That's not insignificant.

→ **Stage 3**, emergent, was about 49%. That's almost half of the organizations that reported.

→ **Stage 4**, structured, was about 28%. These results are improving, but this is less than a third of all companies

→ **Stage 5**, integrated, was only 4%.

→ **Stage 6**, user-driven, was 0.4%.

Note that less than 5% of respondents were at the two highest levels, but NN/g adds an important caveat to their survey results.

I think it's worth including this call out in its entirety here:

> *Stage 3 (Emergent) was by far the most common stage in our dataset — 49% of respondents were placed in that stage. However, that doesn't mean that most organizations in the world fall into that category.*

01. https://www.nngroup.com/articles/state-ux-maturity-quiz/

> *UX practitioners from around the world responded to this survey, but we believe that they were mostly people who have regular UX exposure (for example, NN/g newsletter subscribers and people who follow UX-related tags on social media). That fact suggests that these quiz respondents were not representative of all organizations (a selection bias).*
>
> *As a result, we suspect that there could be many very low-maturity organizations that are not captured by this data because they don't know or care about UX maturity. (This type of result is called a floor effect.)*
>
> *The selection bias is likely to primarily impact the number of respondents and resulting trends for stage 1 and stage 2 organizations.*

Even these scores, which are likely skewed higher than actual results, tell us that about two-thirds of all organizations that responded were still on the lower side of the maturity scale. More than a quarter of respondents were still in the middle. The fact that most teams were far from the top means that overall, most teams still have lots of work to do.

Regardless of how you interpret these results, it's safe to say that most respondents could stand to improve. 90%! Statistically, the odds are good you're dealing with low maturity at work daily.

What does low design maturity mean for UX teams?

But what does this mean for UX professionals, especially individual contributors with little authority to mandate process change? How does low design maturity affect you day to day?

It means those symptoms we highlighted at the beginning of this chapter are likely something you're seeing daily. If you're still in school, know this is what you can expect.

If you're an individual contributor, the odds are good that you won't be able to change the entire organization's culture. However, you can still improve how you work with your core team, and you definitely can still deliver great work.

What does this design maturity model mean for us?

It's essential to distinguish between UX as a job function and UX as Don Norman initially defined it–The definition we discussed at the beginning of the book. UX is simply the experience a user has with a company's goods or services.

Remember that building great software is a team sport, and improving the user experience requires more than wireframes and visual design. The entire team plays a significant role.

For me, these maturity levels aren't just about the number of UX professionals on a team, the number of tasks the UX team is given, or at what point in the overall process the UX team provides input.

We can't reach a higher level of design maturity until everyone we work with understands that they also play a massive role in improving the experience a user has. And, like it or not, that job is left to us.

Know that low design maturity does not mean bad.

Ignore your gut reaction that wants to tell you that low design maturity is inherently bad news. Don't assume the people who run low design-mature teams are dumb or hate UX. That's generally not the case.

Ending up on a low-maturity team doesn't mean the end of the world. And it doesn't mean you have to quit. Even if your team never makes it past stages three or four, don't let anyone tell you that you can't deliver outstanding work on low-maturity teams.

Tips to improve your situation

Before we jump into a few problem scenarios and discuss ways to improve how we work, I want to stress that our goal here is not to improve how everyone works within the entire company or the organization. This chapter aims to improve how we work with our core team. Specifically, our goal is to ensure that we can do our job well, given our constraints. No more. No less.

You may need to change your mindset

The first thing to consider is that this problem often requires a shift in our mindset and approach. In a perfect world, our team would have established processes and followed what we might consider "the right" way to build software. But since this isn't likely the case, it will fall on us to take the lead and help our core team get there.

I don't believe that anyone wants to build crap. Most people want to do great work. First, it's essential to recognize that our team is most likely eager to work with us to improve things. They may just need a nudge in the right direction.

Take a look inward

Before trying to change how our team works with us, it's a good idea to take a step back and reflect on how we're handling the low-maturity situation we've found ourselves in.

It's easy to get caught up in a cycle of blame and point fingers at team members we think are not working the way we want them to. However, improving the way that we work with our team requires us to move past this mindset and adapt to the crappy hand we've been dealt.

This self-reflection also involves acknowledging the limits of our influence. In large organizations or teams set in their ways, the power to make even the slightest change might be beyond our reach. Recognizing this isn't a sign of defeat. And it doesn't mean that there's no point in trying. What's important is that we understand where our efforts can be most impactful. We need to identify areas where our actions can bring about even the slightest improvements.

Addressing these issues is about setting realistic expectations for ourselves and understanding that we won't be able to transform the entire organization. While we may be unable to change everything, our efforts can still significantly impact our immediate team and users.

Lastly, it's important to recognize when the effort to make change is taking a toll on our mental health. And it's important to recognize when it might be time to just go with the flow for a little while. Sometimes, a job is just a job, and you need to get paid. There's nothing wrong with that.

Assume positive intent

Don't misconstrue my advice to assume positive intent as apologizing for bad actors. You may run into these types, and these people should be held accountable.

But remember that your team is full of humans who face the same problems you face. They are likely under the same pressures you're under. And they're going to react the same way you might react. We all have bad days.

Your team consists of people who are just as imperfect as you are. Understanding this and meeting them where they are is essential to improving your collaboration.

In *Chapter 3*, we talked about empathy for our team. This empathy is critical here, especially when we aren't happy with how our team works. It's important not to assume the people on our team are out to get us.

Assuming positive intent is about giving our team the benefit of the doubt. And we must believe that, despite all the challenges and inefficiencies, everyone is doing their best given their constraints.

It's easy to get frustrated and blame our team. Assuming positive intent helps shift the focus to collaboration. It helps us see beyond the surface-level chaos and recognize that our team members might be trying to navigate the mess just like us.

If we approach our team this way, we're more likely to engage in meaningful collaboration and work to find solutions rather than focusing on being defensive.

When we start with the assumption that everyone is doing their best and has the team's best interest in mind, we interact differently with our teammates. This reframe will lead to more positive and productive relationships.

All of that is to say you shouldn't let yourself be taken advantage of, let yourself be gaslit, or stay in a toxic environment that is actively trying to undermine you. No job is worth sacrificing your mental health.

You may be unlucky and find yourself on a team full of misogynists, racists, sexists, ageists, ableists, and anything in between. These people do not deserve the benefit of the doubt. Remember to always look out for number one: you.

Common scenarios and how to deal with them

Below, we'll review a few common scenarios that you may have encountered or will encounter, and discuss your options as an individual contributor without direct authority. You're not alone in facing these challenges.

While we can't cover every possible scenario, the ideas presented here are designed to help you navigate the challenges you'll inevitably face. Understanding and applying these strategies can significantly improve your specific situation. I hope that you will be able to understand how you might improve your specific situation through studying these limited examples.

Scenario One: Stakeholders have an outsized influence

Years ago, I had a particularly difficult stakeholder who consistently created wireframes in PowerPoint, went around the product managers and took these ideas directly to the engineers. Getting direction from an executive, the engineering team took the ideas and ran with them. Before long, this stakeholder had complete control over the product's direction.

This isn't an uncommon scenario on teams with few standards and processes, where a power vacuum is just waiting for someone to fill it.

Let's think about a more generic example.

In this scenario, the design team faces a dynamic where stakeholders like company executives, product managers, or even subject matter experts have disproportionate influence over the software development process. Their involvement might extend beyond providing high-level guidance or feedback, and it starts becoming more directive and prescriptive.

The stakeholders may throw out arbitrary dates based on their idea of the timeline instead of what is realistically possible.

The design team might find themselves adjusting or redoing work to align with this specific stakeholder's feedback over

Mitchell Clements
Senior Product Design Manager

Mitchell shares a story of how exposing design flaws sparked a UX maturity transformation at his former startup, leading to an eventual $1.2 billion acquisition.

In the early stages of my career, I found myself at a small basement startup grappling with low UX maturity. Our product started simple but became more complicated as the company grew. Without regular user research, a design system, or a clear product vision, our user experience deteriorated over time.

To raise awareness of the rising issues, I led the UX team in a comprehensive audit of our product, mapping out every screen and workflow. Using this audit, we created a visually striking collage that showcased the diverse array of button styles within our product. The collage highlighted the fragmented nature of our product and the resulting confusion for our users.

I then presented the shocking visualization at a company-wide all-hands meeting—We had 54 fragmented button styles in our product. There were audible gasps in the room. Some individuals even laughed. How did this happen?

In addition to the button collage, we shared quotes from users highlighting how difficult our product was to use. Then, to drive home the impact of poor UX, we demonstrated the direct financial implications. Our data showed that high support call volumes and lost sales deals that hindered our financial growth were attributed to user experience flaws.

This presentation triggered a series of conversations about investing in our product's user experience, leading us to a four-year transformation. Our efforts included embedding UX designers in every team, conducting more frequent user research, building a design system, and integrating user experience into our product vision and strategy.

The result? That startup grew to 350 employees and eventually reached a $1.2 billion acquisition. The acquiring company attributed the high valuation to the streamlined user experience achieved through our mobile and web platforms.

This journey of transformation taught me three valuable lessons:

01   Transforming a company's maturity isn't an overnight feat. Changing culture is always harder than changing a product. You have to stay committed to the journey if you want to witness the transformation. Measure progress over time.

02   You can't do it alone. It must be a company-wide effort because ultimately every department will impact the user experience and resulting maturity of the company. As a UX team, you must focus on the actionable steps that are within your control and find allies who support your shared vision.

03   For a company to transform its UX maturity, it must have the right values and people. Although we started from a position of low UX maturity, there was a high potential for change. I was lucky to have humble leaders, willing to listen, and committed to doing the right thing. All of us wanted to build the best product for our customers, which meant being committed to creating the best user experience.

UX maturity transformations like this, although rare, are possible. They require dedicated effort and will be challenging, but every step forward is a stride toward success.

other essential data points. The problem is that the stakeholders' feedback can be based more on personal preferences than objective ones.

This disconnect and the stakeholder's influence can lead to situations where stakeholder opinions or personal priorities overshadow user research or even simple UX best practices.

What this means for the UX team

This scenario can tax the design team and lead to a lack of interest overall. It may create a work environment where the team's expertise is undervalued or overlooked.

This situation might not only diminish the quality of the work but also decrease overall job satisfaction and lead to a lack of interest in even trying to deliver good work.

Constant redirection and change of priorities can disrupt the design process and make it difficult to focus on the users. This environment will undoubtedly foster a culture where decisions are more about appeasing stakeholders than delivering user value, which will be incredibly demoralizing for designers passionate about delivering user-centered products.

Tips for improving this situation

Dealing with overbearing stakeholders can take time and effort. It's often hard to know exactly how to handle a stakeholder since this group is nearly impossible to generalize.

Look back to *Chapter 6* and the concepts we covered discussing stakeholder management. Hopefully, this person is on your stakeholder map, and your team has created a communication plan. If so, this is an excellent place to start. But if you haven't done that yet, that's OK.

In general, the tactics we covered in *Chapter* 6 will apply to an overbearing stakeholder, so refer back to the end of that chapter for more general strategies for dealing with stakeholders.

In this scenario, the support of allies is crucial. As a junior individual contributor, you may not have the influence to change an executive or important stakeholder's opinion independently. Forming a plan and working with allies to improve the situation will be your best path forward.

Remember, don't try to go at this alone. It likely won't work.

In this example, the stakeholder is overbearing and controlling, and the chances are good it's happening to everyone, not just the design team. Some product or engineering team members may also feel this is overreach. These are the people you'll want to help organize to fix the problem.

Instead of confronting this overbearing stakeholder in a large group setting, which would likely backfire and not have the intended effect, you'll want to find people who can influence the situation from the sidelines. You'll have a better chance with indirect influence than trying to directly confront this problem.

By now, you should know that your 1:1s may be the most essential tool for fixing many of these problems, and 1:1s are usually where I start. Use your regular 1:1s to get feedback on the overall issues and eventually build a group of allies who can work together to fix this problem from different angles.

There's always the possibility that a stakeholder won't want to have 1:1s with you. If this is the case, you'll need to rely more on your allies and partners to help influence this stakeholder. More likely than not, someone on the team has this stakeholder's ear. Find that person.

If this stakeholder is available, set up regular 1:1s with them to better understand their perspective and where they are coming from. Try to get a sense of their overall vision. Try to understand what issues they are coming up against: Are they under pressure from above? Are they being held to some specific metric in their annual priorities? Are they completely unaware that their job is not to dictate but to inform as a subject matter expert? How new are they to working with software teams? What has their experience been?

These conversations are a great way to build your business literacy. They will allow you to understand the context of the product at a higher level. They might even change your perspective or bring things to light that you hadn't thought of.

These conversations will be a good time for you to understand and hopefully set expectations. What do they expect from the team? Where do they see the design team fitting in? Do they have any sense of how you can help them? Or are they completely unsure about what you do?

If you find that this stakeholder doesn't align with the rest of the team, take this back to your allies and see if there is someone they can bring in to help positively influence the situation. Don't forget that your allies will often have allies of their own.

This point might also be an excellent time to include the stakeholders in some of your activities to show first-hand what you and your team are doing. If you've got an upcoming interview or usability study, invite them to sit in and observe. If the stakeholder is a subject matter expert (SME) with experience doing the work ten years ago, there is a good chance the job has changed. Viewing the current state is an excellent opportunity for this stakeholder to see how his task is done today. And how different it might be from when they did the job a decade ago.

In my example of the overbearing stakeholder at the top of this section, in a 1:1, I found out that this particular stakeholder had a terrible experience working with software teams in the past. This stakeholder had been burned by a team that overpromised and underdelivered, so their approach was to be more hands-on and micromanaged. Our solution was to work to deliver small wins to build trust.

Along with delivering on those quick wins, in our 1:1s, I always candidly discussed how we are working to deliver now, but next time, we wanted to change our method.

It's not about continuously delivering quick wins forever. It's about building trust and improving how we work in the future.

The point of these conversations is to get to know your stakeholders, but part of it is for you to explain what you do, how you think you can help them, and what unique value you can bring to the team if you're given the chance to do your job.

Eventually, they began to trust us and realized we could deliver without micromanaging every task.

Lastly, know which battle is worth fighting. Understanding when you can get your way and when you can't will save your sanity. Since our goal is not to create a UX utopia but to simply improve what we can improve, know that we won't be able to improve absolutely everything every time. And that's okay. Do your best not to stress out over the things you won't be able to control.

Some teams simply won't be able to change everything all at once. However, it might be possible to change little things over time. Make sure that you have a good understanding of your team's capacity for change before you start pushing for change. Pushing for the correct change at the wrong time won't improve anything for you.

Remember that you won't be the only unhappy person when dealing with an overbearing stakeholder. The chances are good that more team members are unhappy with the situation. They might just be waiting for someone to start the conversation.

Scenario Two: There is no North Star vision or roadmap

Some time ago, I was working on software aligned to a more extensive enterprise suite. The trouble was that none of the teams talked or worked together. On a research trip, we observed users hopping back and forth between disparate applications to get their work done because the tools that were supposed to work together simply didn't. It was inefficient and a total waste of time.

If you work in a larger enterprise organization, especially building internal tools, you'll see this siloed software problem regularly. However, the issue of a lack of vision and roadmaps affects even small, tiny startups.

Let's consider a more generic example.

Consider a company experiencing rapid growth. The company's fast-paced growth means they've never crafted a clear North Star vision or a comprehensive roadmap. Projects and features are initiated based on gut feelings, quick market opportunities, or executive whims. The result is a scattergun approach to product releases and features with far-reaching implications.

Imagine the frustration of working in an environment like this. Constantly pivoting and shifting priorities disorient everyone, especially the software team. The lack of a clear vision means that no one understands how these new features contribute to the company's long-term goals.

Since there is no overall strategy, each team has its own priorities and budgets. So teams are working in silos, and the lack of strategic direction leads to a feeling of working from sprint to sprint rather than contributing to something more meaningful and rewarding.

What does this mean for the UX team?

A lack of vision is particularly frustrating for designers because our work is often driven by a passion for creating things that solve big-picture problems. However, lacking a strategic vision means our efforts frequently feel disjointed and lack an overall impact. It's likely that the team struggles with staying motivated and engaged, as the work seems to lack a clear purpose.

The software team's creativity and potential to develop new ideas are stifled in such an environment. The inability to plan long-term or think about the big picture hampers their work. The constant state of change can lead to burnout, dissatisfaction, feeling undervalued, and a general lack of interest in the work. This volatility is a struggle that many of us can relate to.

Regardless of the reason, a lack of vision will eventually impact end users and the business. Without a clear direction, the software will not meet the users' needs, and the company suffer.

Tips for improving this situation

It shouldn't surprise you that relationships will be an essential solution to this problem. Although you may not be able to change the entire organization or get the CEO on board with a new strategic vision, you can help your team be a shining example of how other teams can start planning further out.

These problems aren't "just the way it is."

This is low maturity.

As before, the allies you've built up with your 1:1s will be instrumental in improving how your team works. Instead of using them to change the bad behavior of a stakeholder, you'll use them to help influence other stakeholders to start working differently, like planning further ahead and thinking about the strategic vision or North Star.

Again, the ultimate goal is not to influence the executive leadership team or the C-Suite to change how the entire company works, but you never know what broader impact these allies might be able to make. At the very least, it can't hurt to try.

While having these conversations, talk about planning and having a vision as if it's natural. Start talking like the team would be crazy not to have a roadmap.

If you think you should be talking about outcomes, start talking about outcomes. Ask challenging questions about the outcomes and how the teams are measured. If there are company-wide priorities, ask how these random features the team is being asked to build ties back to those company-level goals.

It is crucial to use every opportunity to emphasize the value of having and sharing a long-term perspective. A North Star vision can significantly enhance the team's work, the overall customer experience, and the company's ultimate success. While some may initially resist, others will see the value and follow your lead.

While trying to convince the team to focus on a long-term vision, work with your product partners to identify key pain points or business objectives that can serve as an informal interim focus for you and your core team. This short-term focus may provide a sense of purpose, even if only for your direct team.

It'll take some time to see meaningful change, so in the short term, focus on delivering quick wins to build trust with the larger team. Without a big picture, concentrate on achieving small wins that align with what you perceive as the company's goals. If you're strategic about the smaller wins, you may be able to start building a case for the importance of a structured roadmap when you show how you've tied it all together.

The idea isn't to keep delivering quick wins indefinitely. As you're talking with stakeholders or the larger team, your goal should be clear: to tie the work to a more meaningful strategic plan over time. This is where a structured roadmap becomes crucial.

If you have data to show how a lack of vision affects users, this can be a powerful tool in convincing stakeholders that something needs to be fixed with the current process. The power of evidence can be a game-changer in these situations.

In my example with the siloed teams, we used our research findings that showed users inefficiently hopping between systems to align the various tools into a more cohesive family of products over time that talked to each other and ended up being a more fluid experience for users.

This information is something your leadership team needs to know. Data like this can be a powerful tool when persuading them to take a more strategic direction, especially when it highlights how misaligned the teams are today.

If your efforts to influence the larger team to craft a strategy or plan aren't working, it will still be worth doing this on your own or with your PM based on your knowledge. Reviewing this information will allow you to take your work back to various stakeholders in meetings, show your vision, and ask for feedback. If it doesn't fit with the leadership team's vision, why not? If not, why don't they have their own vision?

It'll be an excellent opportunity to understand why this type of thing doesn't exist and how you might understand how to make it work going forward.

Often, our team members need something to look at before giving solid feedback. Go into these conversations, saying, "This is what I believe to be true based on what I know. Is this wrong? If it's wrong, can you help me understand how it's wrong?"

If the people you're talking with seem to be on board with creating a vision, you can offer to facilitate a workshop to align the team on a clear vision statement.

You're starting to show that you are the local authority on strategic planning. Tying the more minor features and smaller wins together into a central plan and vision shows first that it's possible and second that you're a good person to keep doing it.

You're setting yourself up as an example others can follow, which might lead to promotions and a more prominent role in helping with the strategy.

Scenario Three: Engineers prioritize what's easy for them

I've worked on small teams. I've worked on large teams. I've worked with startups. I've worked in colossal enterprise organizations. It's hard to generalize most things, but when it comes to software engineers, there is something I've found to be accurate time and time again: Engineers want to write as few lines of code as possible.

This isn't a bad thing! We want our engineering partners to opt for efficiency and simplicity. But sometimes, when the UX team doesn't have sufficient sway or influence, this can lead to the things the UX team cares about being ignored.

In this final scenario, let's look at an organization where the engineering team often opts for easier and quicker solutions to implement from a technical perspective over any other concern. While it's efficient when it comes to coding and deployment, this approach often overlooks the complexities and nuance a great experience requires.

Users end up with functionality that technically works but is cumbersome to use, and that's a huge problem when it comes to commercial software. This means that customers are less willing to pay for these services, which will decrease sales and profits in the long term.

Prioritizing what's easy for engineering is more pervasive on the internal IT side of the industry, where software is seen as a cost center, users tend to be an afterthought, and cutting costs is the name of the game.

Even here, there is the potential for decreased efficiency and longer time on task than is necessary. The result is a product that works–but just barely. Design and tech debt the teams sweep under the rug until later become more significant problems for a future team to worry about.

What does this mean for the UX team?

It can be painful watching your carefully crafted designs, based on hours of research and effort, being diluted for the sake of engineering ease. This scenario can lead to a feeling that the UX team's insights and expertise are being sidelined.

The team may feel their role is more about putting out fires rather than being proactive problem solvers. The constant effort to retrofit an experience into a product that's already been engineered to make a developer's life easier can be exhausting.

It's tough to stay passionate about your work when you feel like your primary role is to always bend to the whims of the engineering team.

Tips for improving this situation

Most people you work with aren't happy building junk. This problem can happen for many reasons, and getting the root cause is an essential first step. Again, 1:1s, where you can have private discussions with individual team members, will be our secret weapon. In this case, we need to spend time with the engineering team to determine the deeper issues.

I've had engineers take a condescending attitude toward the UX team in the past–I've heard all the jokes about crayons and drawing pictures all day. This attitude can be frustrating, to be sure, but in this case, likely, the people doing it don't understand how much your work impacts their work.

1:1s are good opportunities to discuss how your work adds value and makes their job easier by ensuring things are built right the first time. I've never met an engineer who enjoyed refactoring code, so explain how your upfront work saves them from potential refactors later.

The UX team may not be working as efficiently as the engineering team would like. They may view UX as a roadblock– They have to wait too long to receive an answer from the UX team, so the engineers simply choose the best option from their perspective that they feel is correct.

They may not fully understand the specs or know how to interpret wireframes. If there is miscommunication between the engineering and UX teams, they may not realize anything is wrong if the UX team isn't around to tell them it's wrong.

One of the best ways to combat this is to include the engineering team early and often, preferably before you start designing anything. I have always enjoyed getting in a room and brainstorming ideas with an engineer early. These co-design sessions give them insight into how we work, give them a sense of ownership over the process, and help get them to buy into the solution early, which means they're less likely to cut corners or give pushback later.

Something I always have my UX teams do is attend as many Scrum ceremonies as possible: these are regular meetings in the Scrum framework, such as Sprint planning, backlog refinement, daily standups, sprint demos, and especially sprint retrospectives. By being present and engaged in these meetings, you can contribute to the team's understanding and decision-making, and be available to answer questions the minute they come up. If you have the capacity, this is a great way to be seen and be available to answer questions the minute they come up.

Engineers generally like getting feedback early. The sooner they receive feedback, the easier it is to change because waiting until the last minute makes it much harder to make a change.

Being present and available helps you build a positive relationship with your engineers, but it also lets you keep your ear to the ground to catch issues early. You may find that different teams are approaching problems differently. You can help facilitate conversations across teams if you work in a big organization.

The engineers may face unrealistic deadlines from the product team or other stakeholders. If this is the case, they likely aren't happy about the situation either. But they're forced to deliver this way over their internal objections. These unrealistic deadlines can lead to rushed work, increased stress, and a decreased focus on quality, negatively impacting the UX team.

If this is what is happening, see if there is data to support the fact that this experience is hurting the bottom line. If customers aren't happy, the business will suffer, which puts the overall product and team at risk.

If you have the data to back this up, now is an excellent time to make the rounds and discuss this problem with your product partners and stakeholders in your regular 1:1s. Let them see that while it may be faster to ship a product this way, the result, in the long-term, is going to hurt the business.

If you can find allies while having these conversations, you may be able to have them help influence how the engineering team's deadlines are determined. You may help give the engineering team more time to build higher-quality products.

Or the engineering team may not realize that this is hurting end users. They may not even know what end users are trying to do or how this affects the overall experience.

You could educate the engineering team on the users' problems and how this software can help them, as well as explain how the current state needs to catch up. You can also work to sell them on your future vision for the tool. I've often found that seeing a future vision excites the engineers about their work today.

When working on a previous product, the UX team often got weird questions and pushback from engineers. We found them ignoring designs and simply shipping what they wanted. We talked to the engineers and found that we had a real problem: they did not understand what they were building.

I spent about an hour once a month reviewing a new business process and answering questions from my engineering team about the product and the problems we were solving. We reviewed the current state and what our eventual future state would look like, and we explained how each feature fits into the overall roadmap.

We also took an engineer on each research trip as a note-taker. They saw firsthand how the users worked with the software we built and how much room there was for improvement.

Our goal was to get the engineers excited and passionate about the software we were all building–together. And it worked! You can read a detailed case study about this problem on my website.

One of the problems we found on this team was that engineers were cutting corners. Not because they were lazy but because they didn't have an efficient way to share and distribute code across seven pods of nearly 80 engineers on two continents.

Our solution implemented a design system that standardized components across the various engineering teams. Not only did this enable the team to standardize how they built the software, but it also standardized the look and feel of the product.

Having a production-ready code that's available for everyone to see, using something like Storybook.JS, which is a platform that allows engineers to view all of the production-ready components in one place, also made it easy for the UX team to audit components, find discrepancies and address them sooner.

The result was that the engineering team was almost as excited about the work as the UX team. After this, getting them to want to ship high-quality software was easy. And we made it easy for them to build it. It was a win–win for everyone.

Think Long-Term, be persistent and adapt

When advocating for change, your team's capacity to change is essential to keep in mind. Some teams will be able to handle more change than others. Make sure that you understand what your team can handle. Be realistic about what you will or won't be able to change. If you find that your team can only change one or two small things at a time, then focus on changing those small things and save the rest for later.

Pushing for more significant change if your team doesn't have the capacity to change only hurts your credibility and diminishes your overall influence for future change. There will always be time for change.

As we said in *Chapter 2*, work is like an infinite game. Building great software is not a sprint. The changes we want to make will never happen overnight.

But keep at it. Keep the team informed in your 1:1s, and keep working with your allies. Your team may be resistant to change at first. Some people might push back, and others won't see the value of your selling.

Changing how your team works with you may take months or years. Change takes time, especially in organizations with low operational maturity. Stay patient, persist, and continue demonstrating your value to the team. If you do that consistently, slowly but surely, you will bring about the change you want.

Sometimes, these strategies won't work

While we've explored several common scenarios and strategies to address them, it's important to remember that every team and situation is unique. The challenges of low maturity can manifest in countless ways, and there's no one-size-fits-all solution.

You may find that no matter what you do, you simply can't change how your team operates. Not every team will be open to change, and sometimes, like it or not, you'll find a certain type of person who simply isn't worth the effort. Unfortunately, a single person can sometimes ruin everything for everyone else. It's frustrating, but sometimes you cannot do anything about it.

You have a few options when it comes to these scenarios; believe it or not, you have a lot more power here than you may think, even if you don't ultimately change how your team works.

First, recognize the situation for what it is. Assuming you can't get your team to deliver great work, look on the bright side– You're still getting paid.

Many designers get hung up on their teams' not working as efficiently or effectively as possible. Their teams waste time building things no one wants. This certainly isn't ideal, but it could be a lot worse.

I've talked to many designers who say that the concepts we discussed in this chapter are more than they feel they should be doing, and they can't wait to jump ship. I don't blame these people, and I completely empathize with them. I've been in their shoes more times than I like to admit.

If you can afford to quit, then by all means quit. But unfortunately, not everyone has the luxury of quitting without another job lined up. If this is you, look at this as an opportunity to do the bare minimum, keep getting paid, and use this current job to finance your job hunt. I won't fault you for that.

Every designer is different, and every team is different. Every team's capacity to change will depend on any number of factors that may be within or outside of your control. Only you know what will or won't work. And only you know when these things are worth doing and when it's time to move on. Don't let anyone judge you for that. Know your limits: Recognize when a situation is beyond your ability to change, and be prepared to make tough decisions about your career if necessary.

Remember, your primary goal is to improve how you work with your core team, not to transform the entire organization single-handedly. By focusing on what you can influence, you can make meaningful improvements even in challenging environments.

Ultimately, working in a low-maturity environment can be an opportunity for growth. The skills you develop in navigating these challenges—relationship building, strategic thinking, and resilience—will serve you well throughout your career, regardless of where that path may lead.

Not every battle needs to be fought; sometimes, doing your best within your given constraints is enough. Your team's maturity level doesn't determine your worth as a designer.

Chapter 08

The Value of Courageous Followership

We often talk about leadership and the importance of great leaders. But what about the people who follow great leaders?

General Patton would have lost the Battle of the Bulge if it hadn't been for the soldiers in the foxholes.

Martin Luther King wouldn't have made an impact without the thousands of people who protested racial discrimination.

John F. Kennedy's dream of reaching the moon would not have been possible without the countless men and women who worked behind the scenes to make it happen.

Leaders get most of the attention, but great followers make things happen.

There's a near-constant focus on leadership in the world of business. Leadership gurus host seminars, conduct workshops, write books, and teach courses dedicated to molding leaders, celebrating their achievements, and dissecting their brilliant strategies.

However, in this leader-centric worldview, there's a crucial element that often goes unnoticed: The followers. These countless, usually nameless, faceless individuals are the unsung heroes who do the lion's share of the work that brings about the successes of celebrated leaders. Their role is not just significant but indispensable. It's time we acknowledge and appreciate their contributions and remove the stigma of being a "follower."

While leaders often get all the credit, followers are in the background–in the weeds–getting their hands dirty, ensuring things get done.

In this chapter, we'll spotlight these nameless folks–the individual contributors. We'll explore the vital role of followership in any successful team and how you can use these concepts to become a more effective leader if that's the route you want to take.

As we discuss these concepts in this chapter, it might sound familiar. It will sound like things you've heard related to concepts like "leadership behaviors" or "managing up."

I made an episode on my show about managing up a while back. Managing up is the idea that you can influence your superiors and the decisions they make. A friend tagged Dr. David Leitner, who replied, "This sounds a lot like followership." [01]

"Followership?"How had I never come across this term before? After a quick chuckle, thinking this word was a joke, I

---

01. https://www.beyonduxdesign.com/episode/23-mastering-the-art-of-managing-up

immediately googled it. I was blown away by how many great insights there are for a word I had never encountered before.

What is followership?

You're probably sick and tired of seeing everyone talk about "leadership," but the chances are good you've never heard the term "followership" before.

An article from Forbes points out that when you visit Google Scholar, you'll find over five million articles on "leadership." Fewer than 35,000 articles on "followership" exist as of 2024.

If you're anything like me, you giggled a bit the first time you heard this term, thinking it was entirely made up. But it's not a made-up word. It's a fundamental concept that can guide you quite a bit as you progress throughout your career, especially as an individual contributor.

Eventually, I had the opportunity to interview Dr. David Leitner, Ph.D., professor of leadership, strategy, and politics at Bar-Ilan University. This is how "Dr. D" defines Leadership: [02]

> *"Followership is the decision to ascribe to a process that supports and furthers the manifestation of a mutually defined purpose."*

As Dr. D pointed out in our conversation, notice there is no reference to a "leader" for a follower to follow. Simply put, Followership is when you believe in a future vision and do what is needed to help get the team there.

Things we believe in could be specific and concrete, like JFK's vision to put a person on the moon. Or it could be more abstract, like fighting for racial justice, where there may be no clear finish.

---

02. https://www.beyonduxdesign.com/episode/45-unpacking-the-unsung-role-of-follower-ship-with-dr-david-leitner

In our talk, Dr. D gave an example of how there doesn't have to be a clear leader for a follower to rally around. He used the concept of democracy, where there may be political leaders, but democracy is an abstract ideal that we all subscribe to. Who leads "democracy?" No one.

Leadership vs. Followership

Leadership doesn't exist in a vacuum. It's a concept that is inherently tied to followership. For every great leader, countless followers believed, supported, and executed the vision. General Patton had his soldiers at the Battle of the Bulge. Martin Luther King Jr. had the marchers and activists who shared his dream. JFK had the team at NASA working to put the first person on the moon.

The common misconception that followers are simply subordinates waiting for their turn to lead–or worse, passive underlings with no ambition–is far from the truth. Influential leaders need effective, courageous followers to achieve their goals. Followership is not about blind obedience but active engagement, critical thinking, and a willingness to challenge a leader's decisions when necessary. In fact, followers often play a crucial role in the decision-making process, providing valuable insights and perspectives that leaders may not have. It's about being a proactive part of the team, and it's a role that requires as much skill and dedication as leadership.

Even leaders follow something. Find a leader who doesn't follow someone or something. Managers always have a supervisor above them. Even CEOs follow customers, the market, their board of directors, or shareholders. In theory, the leader of a country follows the country's constitution or the ideals it sets forth.

Great leaders need great followers, but great leaders also evolve from great followers because they are followers themselves.

Why is followership important?

Followers are the backbone of any team or organization. They are the people who do the work to turn ideas into reality, the ones who make a leader's vision come to life. Without them, even the greatest ideas will never come to fruition. But good followers are not just there to follow orders.

Followers play a pivotal role in shaping the culture of a company. Their actions and attitudes can influence everyone on the team. If they're positive and engaged, it can help the whole team function smoothly. Conversely, unhappy followers can bring productivity to a standstill. Their influence is so significant that the team's overall morale and productivity can be significantly affected by their feelings about the team's current state. This underscores the immense responsibility and influence that comes with being a follower.

And because there are usually far more followers than leaders, they bring diverse ideas to the team. This diversity helps the team develop new and better ways to do things. Different perspectives can lead to new ideas and solutions that the smaller leadership team may have never thought of independently.

Change usually means new ways of doing things, changing established processes, or shifting the company's overall vision or business model. Making changes is often challenging for even the highest-performing organizations. Followers play an important role in enabling change.

When a company decides to try something new, followers work on it daily. Followers implement change.

Followers are close to the action, so they see firsthand whether or not these changes are working. They can quickly tell if something isn't going right and give feedback to address problems early. Being on the front lines is incredibly important because it helps the organization avoid more significant issues later and makes process changes that much smoother.

Since followers are the ones doing the actual work, their support and buy-in are critical for the change's success. If they're on board and optimistic about the changes, it makes it more likely that things will go well. If not, good luck!

Followership is crucial to any team's success. Followers are not just in the background; they make important things happen daily. Great followers help leaders do more and strengthen the whole team. Even the best leadership team couldn't accomplish much without effective followers.

Characteristics of a good follower

've been lucky throughout my career that my teams have mostly been made up of generally very effective designers. While I hadn't discovered the concept of a "courageous follower" yet. I intrinsically knew what it meant.

Certain people on my teams were people I knew I could count on. These were the people who didn't need every detail explained to them. They didn't come to me the second a new problem popped up. They took the general direction and high-level ideas and ran with them. If someone on the team needed help, they did their best to bring everyone up. Setbacks were not seen as blockers but obstacles to overcome.

When they needed something from me or someone above me, their requests were always well articulated and clear.

Contrast this with some of the people I've worked with over the years who were the opposite. These people often needed very specific instructions. These weren't the type of people to translate a high-level idea into a meaningful outcome. They frequently had a defeatist attitude and were usually very cynical.

Which type would you rather be?

Robert Kelley was one of the first to bring this idea of followership into the larger public conversation. In 1988, he wrote an article titled "In Praise of Followers," which he later turned into a book.[03]

In his article, Kelley listed four essential traits that all effective followers share:

- ✓ They manage themselves well.
- ✓ They are committed to something outside themselves.
- ✓ They build their competence and focus their efforts.
- ✓ They are courageous, honest, and credible.

Interestingly, these four traits all tend to be similar to what you hear when people talk about "leadership behaviors." They're also very similar to what we hear about "managing up."

The interesting thing about leadership and followership is that the behaviors are indeed close since they are two sides of the same coin. Because great leaders are great followers, and great followers can also be great leaders in training.

Let's investigate these four traits and see what makes an effective follower. We'll see how we can apply this to our work as UX professionals.

Good followers manage themselves well

It may seem counterintuitive, but effective followers manage themselves and their priorities well. If you think about this, it

---

03. https://hbr.org/1988/11/in-praise-of-followers

makes sense. Leaders often have many things to do that don't involve direct management of their team's day-to-day work. So they appreciate a team that can take on a task and run with it. They appreciate it when they can trust a team to get things done without having to micromanage every aspect of their work.

Not surprisingly, ineffective leaders will not appreciate these types of employees and prefer a group of "sheep" to control.

Effective followers organize their work and time effectively, set their own goals, and make plans to achieve them. They don't wait for someone else to tell them what to do; instead, they figure out how to finish their work on time.

Self-managed followers are also good at dealing with problems on their own. If something goes wrong, they don't panic and quickly bring in a superior to fix their problems. They'll think about the best way to solve the problem and then do it themselves. This ability to manage stress and solve problems is incredibly valuable to the entire team, especially when leaders have other things they need to do.

Product Managers often capture ideas and features in user stories in Rally or tickets in Jira. You may find yourself without clear direction, but the work needs to get done, often with little guidance from others. As UX professionals, taking an idea and running with it is just part of the job.

Commitment to the organization and something bigger

When I started my UX career, I must admit I didn't have a burning passion for UX Design. In fact, I didn't know much about it other than that designing mobile apps seemed like a pretty sweet job.

Great leaders evolve from great followers because they are followers themselves.

Over time, though, I did discover my passion for building enterprise software. I found immense joy in helping people do their work more efficiently. It was a deeply fulfilling experience to see them finish their work stress-free, enabling them to leave work on time and enjoy their evenings with their families.

UX professionals usually get into this industry because they're interested in the big-picture aspect of the work. They generally embrace the idea of user-centered design, so this commitment to something bigger is usually something most UX professionals intrinsically possess.

Effective followers are deeply committed to a cause they believe in. They often believe in what the organization is doing and want to help it succeed. They believe in the work not out of loyalty to a specific organization or any one person specifically but because they see the organization as a way to realize their goals.

This singular passion is often enough motivation to self-manage and keep on top of work without someone ordering them to do it. It can help make their work feel more meaningful and rewarding. Courageous followers work not just for a paycheck but to make a positive impact.

That said, it's an unfortunate reality that you won't agree with everything your team wants to do. An effective follower will speak up when they disagree, but an effective follower will also realize that once their piece has been said, it's time to commit.

Effective UX professionals will balance things like their desire to create positive user outcomes with the needs of the business and meet somewhere in the middle. If they can't make this work, they might find a new team that aligns better with their values instead of actively working to undermine a mission they don't align with.

LET'S HEAR FROM THE EXPERTS

 Dr. David Leitner PhD
Followership, Leadership, and Strategy Educator

Dr. D shares insights on how to apply strategic followership. By understanding organizational goals and speaking up strategically, we can become key players in our team's success.

As someone who has spent years consulting on strategy and advocating followership, I've seen firsthand the incredible impact strategic followership can have on teams and organizations.

It's not just about playing a supporting role - it's about engaging strategic thinking, building trust, and a bit of thoughtful chutzpah in how you contribute.

For UX designers navigating their employment journey, understanding how to practice strategic followership can set you apart. In a field driven by user-centered design, focusing on strategy is everything.

But what exactly is strategic followership?

At its core, strategic followership is about aligning yourself with the vision of the leader and the needs of the organization while thinking critically about how you contribute to that vision.

It's the ability to support leadership in a way that not only makes their job easier but also adds immense value to the team. You're not just following orders; you're following intention and purpose.

In UX, this can look like taking the initiative to solve problems that fall outside the immediate scope of your role in support of the overall strategic vision. Strategic followers are proactive, anticipating challenges and bringing solutions.

When you engage in strategic followership, you help prevent the disconnect between leadership and the team. You become a translator of sorts—fluent in both design and business language.

Let me give you an example. I was guiding a growing tech startup with their strategic process. They had a small UX team and the leadership struggled with incorporating UX into their broader product development strategy.

One of the UX designers, Sarah, saw this as an opportunity to step up as a strategic follower. She initiated conversations with product managers and leadership to make UX more visible in product discussions.

Sarah showed how a strategic approach to UX could speed up the development process, reduce revisions, and ensure better user adoption.

Her role was pivotal in getting leadership to utilize UX to improve competitive advantage. She was not a "leader" but by being a strategic follower, she was able to lead from within, influencing decisions and shaping outcomes.

I suggest engaging in strategic thinking with thoughtful chutzpah.

Ultimately, followership is a choice.

If you make that choice, remember, it's about understanding and supporting the bigger picture. What are the organization's objectives? How does your work contribute to vision? This mindset shift positions you as a key player in the team's success.

And, don't be afraid to speak up - strategically.

This is where that thoughtful chutzpah comes in. When you see an opportunity to add value, take it. Your voice matters In the end, strategic followership is about engaging in a way that amplifies your impact. It's about understanding the strategy, then supporting leadership with confidence and purpose.

Building skills and making a big impact

Committed followers without much skill won't get very much done, and they know it. When people are committed to a higher purpose and believe in the vision, they're more likely to want to learn, grow, and improve without anyone asking them to.

They won't wait for the next mandated training course. They'll seek ways to improve, like reading, courses, learning new tools or research methods, or asking for feedback on where to improve.

Self-improvement is for more than their benefit. It drives their desire to achieve that higher purpose for the organization. By improving themselves, it helps the whole team get there faster.

Because followers are on the ground and closest to the work, they'll see problems before anyone else does and speak up. They'll try to solve the problem without being told to do it. However, effective followers won't do extra work just to appease their boss. If they are overworked, they will say so and only take on as much as they can realistically achieve.

Courageous, honest, and credible

Traits like courage, honesty, and credibility are commonly linked with effective leadership. However, it's important to note that these qualities are equally essential for followers. Contrary to the classic idea of followers as passive, effective followers play a proactive role and often exhibit these characteristics, making them influential members of the team in their own right.

Effective followers are fearless in speaking their minds. They share their ideas and opinions, even if they differ from what others think, especially their supervisors or stakeholders. They're not scared to ask tough questions or bring up problems. Speaking up is vital because it can help the team avoid mistakes or find better ways of doing things.

Bravery and honesty make us credible. People take us seriously when they know we're not just saying what others want to hear. When we speak up because we believe in what we're saying, our team members notice. This makes credible followers valuable members of the team. Their courage and honesty can inspire others to be open and honest.

Because of this, a courageous follower will hold their leaders accountable. For instance, if those leaders are seen as having conflicts of interest or not working towards the same goals, a courageous follower will hold that leader accountable. Holding a leader accountable could involve initiating a respectful and constructive conversation about the issue, or proposing alternative solutions that align with the team's goals, or reporting the concern to the proper party.

Effective followers aren't mindlessly following orders from above. If those leaders are seen as having conflicts of interest or not working towards the same goals, a courageous follower will hold that leader accountable.

Thinking back to the last chapter, where we discussed low maturity, I hope you can see how these traits can directly improve your team's work.

The vital role of UX professionals as followers

It's important to understand that every organization, even yours, needs effective and courageous followers. Seeing yourself as a courageous follower is critical to understanding the value you bring, even in an individual contributor role.

Your position on the team is much more than just pushing pixels around an artboard. It's actively contributing to the collective goal of creating exceptional experiences. It's helping your stakeholders and product partners understand the value you bring. Your role is integral to the operation of the entire software team. Understanding the concepts behind being an effective follower will amplify your impact.

Detailed execution of the mission and vision

A core responsibility is translating the vision senior leaders and stakeholders have developed into tangible artifacts for the team to see and interact with. This helps the entire process move forward efficiently. This responsibility is enormous.

This seemingly small responsibility goes beyond a simple "prototype jockey." It requires a deep understanding of the product and the business's vision for the product and service. Your responsibility is to understand these things so that when you craft artifacts, you know deeply what you're building and how it fits into the bigger picture.

As you work on these items, your attention to detail, understanding of UX fundamentals, and ability to internalize and incorporate feedback are all critical.

Whether you realize it or not, you're helping bridge the gap between abstract ideas and practical applications that excite the rest of the team about what they're working on. You shouldn't take this "simple" act of designing for granted.

Shaping Team Dynamics and Culture

Culture can never really take shape from the top down. Culture only really happens from the bottom up. No matter how determined the best leaders may be, followers are the ones who shape the culture of the entire team.

As an IC, your influence on team dynamics and culture is enormous. How you approach collaboration, how eager you are to learn, and how open you are to feedback can make or break the creation of a supportive environment. Your attitude helps shape how the rest of your team will interact with one another.

Positive interactions, willingness to help colleagues, and taking on complex challenges will outsize team morale, especially when dealing with low design maturity.

On the other hand, a reluctance to engage, a negative attitude, and cynicism are contagious. When this negative attitude spreads, it can be hard for anyone to stop.

Embracing your role as a follower includes contributing to a team culture where creativity, respect, and mutual support are the norms. You have more power here than you realize.

Offering ground-level insights and feedback

Your hands-on involvement in different aspects of the product lifecycle, like discovery, user research, meetings, prototyping, or usability studies, equips you with valuable insights the people above you aren't necessarily getting.

You're likely dealing with the day-to-day process of a working software team where leadership might only get sporadic updates cherry-picked by middle managers. You're likely seeing gaps in processes, inefficiencies, or duplicative work senior leaders miss.

It's your responsibility to share these observations with your team and help refine and improve things, resulting in a more efficient process for everyone.

Your role as a courageous follower requires you to be a voice from the ground up to the leadership team. Don't stay quiet!

Facilitating change and supporting team initiatives

How you support, embrace, or implement new processes, organizational changes, or even a product pivot impacts the team's overall success.

Adapting and adjusting to new processes and design directions demonstrates a commitment to the team's overall success, even if you aren't 100% on board. You can ensure that product strategy and scope transitions are executed smoothly and efficiently. Leaders could never do these things on their own.

Effective and courageous followers like you make this possible!

Turn followership into leadership success

You may be struggling to find your footing now. You may find yourself on a team where you aren't respected. You may not be a trusted partner yet. You might feel like you have no control.

A genuinely courageous follower will observe and take in the larger conversations happening around them. They'll work to understand how the tactical things they're being asked to do fit into the bigger picture and how these specific solutions are solving larger business or user problems.

As an individual contributor, embracing your role as a follower means nurturing your potential leadership qualities and gaining valuable wisdom you will use later. Your day-to-day experiences, collaboration with your cross-functional team, and exposure to all the challenges that go along with that will serve as a foundation for developing leadership skills over time. Absorbing these things happening around you will enable you to become an effective leader when the time comes.

Remember that every great leader once started as a follower. The skills, insights, and experiences you gain in your current role lay the foundation for your future success. If you embrace followership and all of the ideas in this book, you're actively preparing for your moment to lead. The qualities of a good follower—adaptability, humility, collaboration, and a sense of purpose—are all traits that will serve you well as a future leader.

Courageous followership is about actively engaging with your work and your team. It's about speaking up, daring to voice your ideas, questioning the status quo, being willing to teach, offering constructive feedback, and leading when the time is right. This will make you a valuable team member now and equip you with the wisdom and confidence to move to leader and beyond later.

As you grow in your career, remember the importance of the relationships you build. Networking isn't only to make professional connections; it builds a mutually beneficial community of peers, mentors, and friends who support and inspire each other to improve. These relationships will be your compass, helping guide you through your career.

Each challenge you face and overcome, each bit of feedback you receive, and each setback is a lesson in leadership. Embrace it!

The future of UX is not in the hands of today's leaders. It's in the hands of courageous followers, just like you, who are shaping their path to leadership, one 25-minute 1:1 at a time.

As you step forward in your career, carry the lessons of this book with you. The humility, empathy, and collaborative spirit you cultivate now will be your greatest strengths as a future leader. You're not just preparing to lead your team's design efforts; you're learning how to inspire and influence your entire team, make a meaningful impact through your work, and ultimately shape the future of our discipline.

Godspeed!

Life gave me lemons, so I wrote a book.

Acknowledgments

Sometimes life throws you curveballs. Usually, you don't get a choice in the matter. They're coming for you whether you like it or not.

The only thing you can do is control how you react to said curveball. I chose to take advantage of lots of free time I didn't expect to write this book. In fact, you probably wouldn't be reading this book without that extra free time neither I nor my family wanted! 😨

In a weird way, I'm thankful for that curveball. So thanks corporate overlords, it looks like you did me a favor!

First, to all my readers and listeners, thank you for joining me on this crazy journey. Your curiosity, engagement, and passion for UX design are what make all of this worthwhile for me. This book is as much yours as it is mine.

Writing this book has been an incredible journey, one that I could not have embarked on without the support, wisdom, and encouragement of many remarkable individuals.

I couldn't have written this book without my incredible and supportive wife Aimee. Thanks for putting up with the loud typing, the ice chewing, and all the late nights. I couldn't have done it without you.

To Linus and Arlo, I know that you only read books with pictures right now, but I hope one day you'll find this book helpful useful.

To my brilliant colleagues in the UX design community, thank you for the stimulating discussions, the shared resources, and the solidarity. This book is richer for your contributions.

A special shout-out to the guests of the Beyond UX Design podcast—your stories and insights have been a wellspring of inspiration and personal growth.

Thank you to my D-Unit people, you have been an infinite source of inspiration and motivation for me. Especially Tibi David, Chris Nguyen, Philip Wallage, Dan Winer, and Aneta Kmiecik. You all have inspired me more than you know.

This book wouldn't be complete without a shout-out to all the friends I've made over the last couple of years on Slack. You know who you are. Thank you for the inspiration. I wouldn't be here without you. 🙏

I have to give a shout-out to the engaging and supportive community on LinkedIn, where the exchanges and feedback have been both enlightening and encouraging. Your engagement and thoughtful comments have been a source of daily motivation for me. It's what keeps me going.

A special thanks to all my Patreon supporters, especially Chris, Sirikhwan, Stacie, Radu, Maigen, Andrew, John Mark, Kevin, Jason, Michelle, and Marti for their continued support over the last year or more. And especially to Chris for being the very first person to help support the show financially. Chris, you'll always be my first!

Last but not least, I extend my thanks to the countless cups of coffee and late-night playlists on brain.fm that have kept me company throughout the writing process. Your fuel has been, both literally and metaphorically, what has kept me going.

Thanks to these editors and reviewers

I would like to call out some specific individuals who have helped with valuable feedback and input.

This book is better because of you!

- → Derek Seibert
- → Julia Debari
- → Andrew Macdonald
- → Hang Xu
- → Kevin Shertz
- → Philip Wallage
- → Mitchell Clements
- → Lennart Nacke
- → Tomi Joshua
- → Abdullah Qureshi
- → Drew Herrema
- → Simonas Maciulis
- → Dr. David Leitner PhD
- → Matthew McPhail
- → Amy Santee
- → Manos Stefanakis

Thank you all for being part of this journey!

Thank you contributors!

I want to express my heartfelt gratitude to the incredible experts who generously shared their insights throughout this book. Their contributions have brought depth and real-world perspective to each chapter.

I'm deeply honored to have worked with such talented individuals, and my sincere hope is that their insights will resonate with you long after you've finished reading.

Yaddy Arroyo
Principal Multimodal AI designer
Yaddy is a specialist in AI UX design, known for creating seamless multi-modal banking experiences. Discover more about her work at *yaddyarroyo.com*.

Christopher Nguyen
Founder UX Playbook
Chris is the brains behind the successful UX playbook, a UX learning platform trusted by 12k+ designers from startups to Fortune 500s. Learn more about his offerings at *uxplaybook.org*.

Dan Winer
Director of Product Design @ Kit
Dan uses his leadership experience to help designers build confidence, do meaningful work and grow their careers. Find out more about his course and newsletter at *designcareer.guide*.

Tim Yeo
Chief Introvert, The Quiet Achiever
Tim is a designer, design leader, and the author of *The Quiet Achiever*. You can learn more about the book and pick up your copy at *www.thequietachievr.com/book*.

Tonja Barlow
Principal Voice User Interface Designer
Tonja is a seasoned UX designer with 16+ years of experience in diverse industries, blending art and technology. Explore her work at *tonja-uxdesign.com*.

Thomas Wilson
Director of Experience + Service Design + Strategy
Thomas is a manager of madness and curiosity crusader, known for his expertise in human-centered Service Design. Learn more about his work at *thomasianwilson.com*.

Mitchell Clements
Sr. Product Design Manager
Mitch is a seasoned Design Leader who regularly shares his insights on career growth, design leadership, and the business value of design. Learn more about Mitch at *mitchellclements.com*.

Dr. David Leitner PhD
Followership, Leadership, and Strategy Educator
Dr. D. is a consultant specializing in Followership, helping teams align through strategic engagement. His work encourages support with strategic thinking and thoughtful chutzpah. Learn more at *drdleitner.com*.

About the author

Jeremy Miller is a veteran Design leader with nearly two decades of experience in the design industry. He is the dynamic voice behind the popular podcast "Beyond UX Design," where he champions the idea that soft skills are crucial in making a truly effective UX professional.

Jeremy's design career began in the early 2000s, with a strategic shift to UX in 2011. Throughout his journey, he has delivered impactful results at both large corporations and startups, while mentoring countless designers along the way.

In 2024, Jeremy joined Edge Kase Design Co., a consultancy dedicated to helping organizations bring their innovative ideas to life. His approach is rooted in the firm belief that you can't build great software without great relationships–a philosophy he enthusiastically shares with anyone willing to listen.

Drawing from his extensive experience and passion for the field, Jeremy continues to inspire and educate through his podcast, consultancy work, and mentorship. His unique perspective blends technical expertise with a deep understanding of the human elements that drive a successful career, making him a respected voice in the industry.

I'd love your feedback

Thanks for reading my book. I sincerely hope you found it valuable. If you did (or even if you didn't), I'd be super grateful if you could spare a minute to leave a quick review.

Reviews help other readers decide if this book is right for them, and they're incredibly valuable to me personally. Plus, your feedback will help shape my next book!

Whether it's a couple of words or a few sentences, every review counts. So if you have a moment, please share your thoughts wherever you like to talk about books online.

Scan Me!
I want to hear from you

Let's stay connected

There's even more content available online. Follow Jeremy on LinkedIn for a daily dose of UX wisdom. And makes sure to subscribe to the Beyond UX Design Podcast wherever you listen to podcasts.

in linkedin.com/in/jmillspaysbills

🌐 beyondUXdesign.com

✉ hello@beyonduxdesign.com

Download five additional chapters today

Unlock additional insights and practical wisdom with five additional bonus downloads.

Designed to complement your journey into UX design, these resources are essential for new designers and career shifters looking for their first UX job.

Kickstart your UX career with expert insights

Use the code **EXTRAS** at checkout!

01   **Why are You Chasing a UX Career?**
Uncover your motivation for pursuing UX design and assess if your personality aligns with the demands of the profession.

02   **The Reality of UX Outside the Classroom**
Uncover the non-linear nature of UX, the realities of working with cross-functional teams, and the need to quickly adapt.

03   **Stop applying and start connecting**
Explore opportunities beyond well-known companies, and develop a network that will benefit your career in the long run.

04   **The Paradox of the Perfect Portfolio**
Learn to tailor your case studies to your audience and approach portfolio creation as you would any UX project.

05   **Will This Team Be a Good Fit For Me?**
Gain insights into evaluating job offers by understanding the role and company culture, ensuring a perfect fit for you.

Scan Me!

to get additional content
BeyondUXdesign.com/extras

Love listening to this show. As a recent bootcamp grad myself, it's so helpful for my post course education to feel immersed in UX and design thinking. A lot of useful advice, with positive vibes!

rytdnn

Jeremy is an excellent podcast host and the guests he chooses are fun to listen to. It's a very engaging show for anyone working or interested in the field of user experience design. Thanks for creating this.

thx_len

This podcast is awesome. 👏 It provides an uplifting/positive but realistic POV on UX design. Great interviews, helpful discussions of skills needed for success, and thoughtful takeaways. 🤓

Texdlew

d keeps it   insig

⭐⭐⭐⭐⭐

emingly flu   Jeremy is great at taking an already human-centered topic and making   just so ref
                   it personal. Plus, he's funny. Well worth the listen.
t balance   **Texdlew**   entually g

Great co   ⭐⭐⭐⭐☆   Very

ightful nu   I really don't understand the intro line 'how is your mom and them'. I   interview
                   got no idea what this means but it is very odd to mention my mom.
As a new   **咕叽咕叽amanda**   who's thin

th are like   giving liste

our podc   it is easily

Scan Me!

For the latest
Beyond UX Design
Podcast episode

CognitionCatalog

Peek behind the curtain of your subconscious

Scan Me!
to get a new
Cognitive Bias
Every Friday

Boomerang Effect

CognitionCatalog »»

Self-Reference Effect

CognitionCatalog »»

Identifiable Victim Effect

CognitionCatalog »»

Acquiescence Bias

CognitionCatalog »»

...e Shedding Effect

...onCatalog »»

Insensitivity To Sample Size
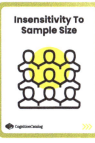
CognitionCatalog »»

Memory Inhibition
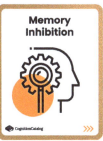
CognitionCatalog »»

Mere-Exposure Effect

CognitionCatalog »»

Subscribe Today!

SHOP NOW AND GET

20% OFF

Use the code **BUXBOOK** at checkout!

Scan Me!

to get your print on
BeyondUXdesign.com/shop

Feeling stuck?

Let's elevate your career together

With 1:1 Coaching!

- 🏆 **Master Relationship Building**
- 🔭 **Shape Product Vision**
- 🪧 **Navigate Team Dynamics**
- 🚀 **Accelerate Career Growth**
- 🛠️ **Expand your Toolkit**
- 🧭 **Thrive in Uncertainty**

What truly distinguishes Jeremy is his dedication to understanding me personally and providing advice that's tailored to my unique path. With Jeremy, I am more than just a mentee; I am a young designer whose voice matters.

Gaozong Y.

Jeremy is very passionate and knowledgeable. We discussed various career paths for UX designers as well as other topics related to continuous education. I highly recommend him.

Armantas Z.

Jeremy was energetic and kind during our chat. He provided pragmatic and thoughtful guidance that I will be using as I traverse my new role. I found him to be very easy to talk to and very humble while leaning on his expertise. I will be connecting with Jeremy again because he was so fantastic!

Matthew M.

Jeremy guided me in laying out my goals and provided clear and insightful portfolio and networking tips. I feel much more confident and motivated moving forward. He was very open to keeping in touch, and overall such an open-hearted individual. Looking forward to learning more from him!

Kaho F.

Scan Me!

to book a
FREE Discovery Call